The Persuasion of Love

Is there a theological Theory of Everything?

Also by John Blakely
(Writing as Peter Longson)
God in the Dark
ISBN 978-1-84952-215-1

What people are saying about
The Persuasion of Love

If we are willing to do as God has done and risk everything for love, then he may be able to surprise us' says John Blakely. This book is an inspiring and poetic meditation on love, desire and grief in the context of Christian faith. Using practical insights from personal suffering, from science and scripture, from theology and from his professional musicianship, John Blakely writes beautifully about how our experiences of love challenge us to expand our thinking and doing in response to the love of God.

Read it with joy, risk everything, and be surprised into action by the depths of God's love in us and for us and for all the world.
The Very Revd Dr David Ison, *Dean of St Paul's Cathedral, London*

The Persuasion of Love is a companion piece to John Blakely's first book, *God in the Dark, Rebuilding faith when bad stuff happens*, published in 2012 by Wild Goose, www.ionabooks.com, under the pseudonym Peter Longson, ISBN 978-1-84952-215-1.

Peter Longson's *God in the Dark* is an exquisitely written exploration of the problem of suffering ... Longson's style is relaxed and poetic ... The book is utterly honest, and his section on the things we say to people when they have had their world rocked by tragedy is essential reading for any who try to care for those who are suffering ... With a mixture of science, theology and philosophy, Longson pulls off an astonishing, deep and coherent argument – by far the best book that I have ever read about the problem of pain. It has a profound conclusion that is deeply satisfying.
Church Times

This book is a valuable addition, from a professional musician, to the theological literature that sees God as an artist or composer, as well as a steady and reliable guide for Christians who genuinely want to take suffering seriously.

Modern Believing

With ruthless logic, deep compassion and a pastoral heart Longson beats a scholarly path through science, theology, philosophy and literature, questioning much of conservative Christian understanding of theodicy. Out of the wreckage he builds something where the world as it is, human life as we experience it and a God of love can reside together. It is essential reading for all who seek to bring the love of God to a world which groans under the weight of suffering and evil.

The Revd Canon Dr John Searle OBE

The Persuasion
of Love

Is there a theological Theory of Everything?

John Blakely

Winchester, UK
Washington, USA

First published by Circle Books, 2019
Circle Books is an imprint of John Hunt Publishing Ltd., No. 3 East St., Alresford,
Hampshire SO24 9EE, UK
office1@jhpbooks.net
www.johnhuntpublishing.com
www.circle-books.com

For distributor details and how to order please visit the 'Ordering' section on our website.

Text copyright: John Blakely 2018

ISBN: 978 1 78904 000 5
978 1 78904 001 2 (ebook)
Library of Congress Control Number: 2018932807

A CIP catalogue record for this book is available from the British Library.

Design: Stuart Davies

Printed and bound by CPI Group (UK) Ltd, Croydon, CR0 4YY, UK

We operate a distinctive and ethical publishing philosophy in
all areas of our business, from our global network of authors to
production and worldwide distribution.

Contents

For my wife Marion, and children Ruth, Andrew and Alison
and their families,
in thankfulness for their love.

Preliminaries

This book is an attempt to play around with the idea that the meaning of the universe is Love. But hubris is an ever-present danger.

As we unwrap this idea and see how it might work out in practice, we shall of course be making many references to the nature and activity of God, and specifically the God who Christians believe is revealed in the person of Jesus. But we'd better be clear: anything we can say is said by mere creatures, and faulty ones at that. Gods we are not, so we'd better not get above ourselves. God, if he is worth knowing, must be allowed to be ultimately unknowable, if that is not too paradoxical a thought. God reveals himself to Elijah as 'a sound of sheer silence' (1 Kings 19:12), and Hab 2:20 advises 'Let all the earth keep silence before him'. And if we do have the temerity to speak, then anything we can say must be provisional and liable to be changed, either by new insights or by the inrush of light that we pray may accompany our transition from this life to the next. In that respect it's not so different from the way scientists do their work: any theory, however revelatory, is provisional and open to being superseded by new data and new ideas that offer a better fit to the facts.[1]

But talk of a theory leads to another danger: that of abstraction. Certainly we must first engage and convince our minds; but if it stops there I think we will have been wasting our time. This is not a theoretical exercise, or something to be indulged in by a small group of people with a particular inclination towards the philosophical or theological. Thinking these thoughts is not the password for access to some spiritual club. If it turns out that there is any sense in the idea that 'the meaning of the universe is Love', then it must change the way we look at that universe – as creation, as the place where we live together, and as the place where, we believe, God has made himself known. And if we look at it differently we may need to act in it differently.

But as long as we are careful to keep ourselves in our place, to avoid intellectual pride and to make sure that we prefer to be practical rather than merely theoretical, then I think we can risk setting out on this journey. After all, love comes with risk, and if risk is refused, then love is excluded, as we shall see.

In this book[2] I hope to show that there is evidence, and some of it in surprising places, for love being the reason for everything, and being in everything. But we have to develop the capacity to see it, and broaden our expectation of what it might be.

1

The Greeks had a Word for It

'When I use a word,' Humpty Dumpty said, in rather a scornful tone, 'it means just what I choose it to mean – neither more nor less.' 'The question is,' said Alice, 'whether you can make words mean so many different things.' 'The question is,' said Humpty Dumpty, 'which is to be the master – that's all.'
(Lewis Carroll)[1]

'The meaning of the universe is Love'
At first glance, this may seem an obvious truth – more platitude than profundity. And if it is true, then in one sense that's all that needs to be said, and this would be a very short book. We would have done no more than stating the obvious. But if we scratch the surface, we may find that things are not quite as straightforward as they first look. And we may find that if we really begin to believe it, it may change everything.

It's not difficult to find plenty of reasons to say that the evidence points in quite a different direction, and we will need to face up to them. And in any case, what are we talking about when we use the word love in such an ambitious context? We may well find ourselves needing to re-evaluate what we mean by it, and it may be that as we pursue this exploration of what we must acknowledge is a dangerously over-used concept, we will be in for a few surprises about what it is and is not, and about where it may or may not be found. And of course it's already a philosophical and theological leap to say that the universe has a 'meaning' at all, and we will need to find some justification for that as we go along.

A hot topic in science over recent years has been the search for a Theory of Everything. Specifically, this would provide a way of reconciling Einstein's Theory of General Relativity (which deals with how things work on a very large scale) with Quantum Mechanics (which deals with how things work on an unimaginably small scale). More generally, a Theory of Everything would claim to do what it said on the tin: to provide, presumably in mathematical terms, a way of expressing a view of reality such that it could answer every question that could ever be asked. Put like that, we would probably be wise not to hold our breath until someone can articulate it. But even if we settle for the more limited and specific aim outlined above, it's difficult to avoid the feeling that it may lie forever just out of reach. Stephen Hawking has said that although he used to believe that it might be possible to find it, he has now changed his mind and thinks it cannot be achieved. Doubtless, though, the search for a Theory of Everything will throw up unexpected discoveries, so that even if the search is ultimately fruitless, the attempt will have been worth it for what is discovered along the way.

In this book I want to suggest that the search for a theological Theory of Everything might be similarly productive. Love casts its net more widely than we might imagine, but is of course fundamental to whatever we might want to say about the Christian faith. The trouble is that it's so much part of the fabric of Christian belief that we may be in danger of not noticing it any more. We have all had the experience of realising that there has been a background noise going on only when it stops. The place of love in Christianity can be like that. If asked, we would say we know it's there, but most of the time it's like the background noise, there but not there, while we focus our active attention on some detail or other. But what might happen if we really were to restore love to its central place? Not theories of the Atonement, nor debates about gender, orientation and ministry, nor attitudes to how we use the Bible. These all have their place, but unless love is central to our thinking and feeling and understanding, we may come to conclusions that are skewed away from God's huge idea. But if love really is what the universe is made of, then that may change everything.

To take a current example. There has been intense debate in the Anglican Communion over issues of women's ministry, and of the place of the gay community particularly in relation to ordained ministry. These controversies summon up great depths of feeling on all sides. This is fine – we should care. But what has been depressing is the way in which the debate has often, though not always, been conducted. At times, love has been notable for its absence. If the non-Christian world sees us acting and speaking in ways that are not first of all guided by love, then we have no right to expect anyone to listen to the message. As Jesus put it, and succinctly, (Jn 13:34-35): 'I give you a new commandment, that you love one another. Just as I have loved you, you also should love one another. By this everyone will know that you are my disciples, if you have love for one another.' The scary corollary of course is that if we don't love, they won't know.

But what is this thing that we are, perhaps too easily, calling love? *'O Tell me the Truth about Love'* wrote W. H. Auden.[2] 'When it comes, will it come without warning / Just as I'm picking my nose?' Well, Auden had his tongue firmly in his cheek, so we should not look for too much revelation in his rhetorical question. But we had better decide what, in a Christian context, we think we are talking about. 'In a Christian context': I laid a trap for myself there. Is the love we are thinking of some special kind of love which is identifiable only when we are talking in 'Christian' terms? Is it some special and new manifestation of something we know about from other contexts, but which has been spiritualised, or de-cluttered from all its usual human associations? I want to suggest that that is not at all the case, and that if the meaning of the universe is love, then that is the only love there is. There is no special Christian love, because all love is God's love. There may indeed be different manifestations of it, and to be sure the first followers of Jesus understood that in the incarnation, life, death and resurrection of this man they had been touched in a new and life-changing way by the love of God. And all who have followed him since know that 'God so loved the world that he gave his only Son' (Jn 3:16). A new kind of love. But that is not quite right: we are looking not so much at a new kind of love, as at a new manifestation of an ages-old love. A new, and, it turns out, the ultimate, manifestation of love. But the question is: is it so new that it bears little or no relation to anything else we might be talking about when we say the word 'love' in any other context? I suggest not. If God is love and has made love the energy of the universe, then there can be no love that does not have God as its source, however hidden it may be, or however marred by human failings. This is a very dangerous idea! We will consider some of those dangers in due course, but first we need to discover whether there is perhaps a linguistic clue in the New Testament that would suggest that indeed 'Christian love' is unconnected to other loves. What perhaps points in that direction is the well-known fact that the New Testament writers even came up with a 'new' word to use for this 'new' love. Well – the word existed already of course, but they used it in a quite new context and to deliver quite new content. But maybe the implications are not exactly what we thought.

The New Testament writers, who had been touched in this new way by the love of God, chose to use the Greek word *agape*, and words derived from that root, for the vast majority of their references to love. There were in fact four words available in the Greek of the time, and they all had different meanings, or indicated the different contexts in which we might come across love. C. S. Lewis famously wrote about them in his book *The Four Loves*, identifying them as Affection (*storge*), Friendship (from the verb *phileo*), Eros, (*eros*, which English has taken directly from the Greek), and Charity (*agape*).[3] In the New Testament there are something like 250 uses of *agape*. There are far fewer words using the root of *phileo*, which can be understood as friendship, for instance in the context of mutual interest. There are hardly any for *storge*, which is affection, particularly in the context of family, and there are none at all for *eros*, which is love in the context of desire, including sexuality.

This accuracy and clarity of the Greek language, which can give us insight into what lies behind the outward appearance, was clearly a wonderful tool for the New Testament writers. In the famous passage in John chapter 21, the risen Jesus is firmly but oh so gently counselling Peter after the disaster of his denial. In most English translations, the painful subtlety gets lost.[4] Twice Jesus asks Peter if he loves him (*agapas*), and Peter, for whatever reasons of shame or perhaps of honesty, can only reply that he loves him with *philia* love. The third time, heartbreaking in his tenderness, Jesus asks only if Peter loves him with *philia* love, and Peter has to reply again that yes, that is the only kind of love that he can acknowledge in his broken relationship with his master. But Jesus still continues with his commission of Peter to feed his sheep, and be the first leader of the church. His *philia* love, which is the best he can do, is good enough for God to work with. Why? Because God is tender, and because God is the source of that love too. He is the source of anything that we can call love. If this conversation is a humiliation for Peter, it is also his salvation, because Jesus is willing to come to him as he is, and where he is, however guilty and remorseful he may be.

Before the New Testament writers got hold of *agape*, it was in fact, in contrast to the other three rather specific kinds of love, a relatively obscure word with no particular overtones. So it is often suggested that this word was chosen so that it could express a completely new concept of love, the love demonstrated by God in his dealings with us, and by us in our response to that love. The idea would be that there are these four kinds of love, but one of them is new, and different, and special, and belongs particularly to God – and to us when we respond to his love. I think this is the implication of C. S. Lewis's book, which to be sure is wonderfully insightful in helping us to understand love's different contexts and manifestations. But the danger is that we put each different love into its own box, and think that they have different sources. And the danger that follows on from that is that we may think that only one kind of love has God as its source, and that only one kind can give us a clue as to his character.

But these demarcations don't really seem to be appropriate when we experience love. It's just love, given and received in the context that it happens to live in. So I want to suggest this quite different approach, and I think it is one that makes sense of the passage we were just looking at. The idea, as I suggested a moment ago, is that there is only one kind of love, because there is only one source of love. There is no love that does not, however dimly, ultimately owe its existence to God, who, John tells us in I Jn 4:16, *is* love. So *agape* was the word for the writers of the gospels and letters to use, for the very good reason that it comes to us with no baggage. It tells us that there is only one love, though we experience it in widely differing contexts. Jesus, in his interview with Peter, wants him to understand that, even if he is only capable, at this lowest point in his life, of *philia* love, that's alright. The love of which he is capable is still a love that has God as its source. By being capable of *philia* love he is in touch with the God who is its source. Or, better, God is in touch with him. *Philia* love is a subset of *agape* love. Or, if you prefer, we could say that in a Venn diagram all those other loves would be contained within the large circle that is *agape* love. *Agape* encompasses all the others. But the others are not outside it. They are within its orbit. They are all made of the same stuff.

The New Testament writers certainly wanted to make a point

by their use of *agape*, and they seem to be aware that this was a new way of talking about love. In another story in John's Gospel, where we see Jesus' humanity in all its painful vulnerability, he joins in the very public mourning for his friend Lazarus. John's stark recollection is that 'Jesus began to weep' (Jn 11:35). The Jewish mourners then comment 'See how he loved him!' They are not, or not yet, aware of the possibilities opened up by the idea of *agape*, and so John has them saying 'See what *philia* friendship he showed towards him!' The move towards using *agape* is conscious and measured, and is initiated by writers and thinkers who were beginning to search for the meaning of Jesus, and particularly the meaning of his death and resurrection. They were bringing a new idea into talk of love, and knew what they were doing. For the new wine of God's love they needed the new wineskin of a new word (Mk 2:22) that would encompass everything.

Perhaps the best-known use of a word from the root of *agape* in the New Testament is in John's affirmation that we noticed a moment ago, that 'God so loved the world that he gave his only Son' (Jn 3:16). It may be worth keeping something about this very direct and disarmingly simple statement in the back of our minds for later, when we begin to look at God's relation to the created order. The verse is often glossed as something like 'God loved everyone so much'. To be sure, the verse continues with good news of eternal life for 'everyone who believes in him', but it seems that John is seeing 'everyone' as part of something much larger in scope, for the word translated as 'world' is the Greek *kosmos*. English has taken that word directly of course, and while the Greek can mean the world and its people, it can also mean the universe. John is developing a big picture of what the good news may encompass, and we will do well to try to do the same.

Though the compiler of a dictionary will have to make the attempt, it is curiously difficult to define love. This might seem a major snag for a book whose subject this is, but all is far from being lost. Though we may not be able to put it into words, the wonderful thing is that we are instinctively able to recognise it. The point is that we know it when we see it, without needing to sit down and debate or analyse. And we see it and sense it when it moves. John latches onto this with his characteristic simplicity that hides the depth of his thought – the art that conceals art: 'Little children, let us love, not in word or speech, but in truth and action. And by this we will know that we are from the truth' (1 Jn 3:18-19). We can only recognise it when it's doing something. In fact I would go so far as to suggest that it only exists at all when it's doing something – if we include within the idea of acting the intention or decision to act in a particular way. *Agape* is not a new kind of love, and certainly not some rarified type that has made an appearance late in the day and rather to our surprise from its home in a disembodied heaven, and towards which we are supposed to ascend by the action of God's grace. *Agape* is much more down-to-earth, and is willing to get stuck in. It is love expressed in a new kind of action, or in a different context. 'God proves his love for us in that while we still were sinners Christ died for us', says Paul in Rom 5:8. Here there is no definition of love as a concept, but two verbs that tell us what it does. God does not tell us about love in abstract words, but shows it to us in action; and in this case the action is ultimate and total self-giving. We know it when we see it. God got his hands dirty doing it.

The same focus on action can be seen in Paul's famous paean to love in I Cor 13:4 ff. 'Love is patient; love is kind', he says. 'Love is not envious or boastful or arrogant or rude.' This passage is understandably used as a reading at countless church weddings, and seems to be incapable of being diminished by frequent use. But, again, our translations can easily obscure an important point. In the English translation I have just used, the description uses only adjectives. But in the Greek, Paul uses only verbs. So it's more a case of 'love acts in a persevering way, behaves with kindness, does not burn with jealousy, does not put on a display of self, does not inflate itself, does not act in a rude way'. In every one of these descriptions, we know it by what it does or doesn't do. There is no attempt to say what love is in the abstract. We are told what it will and won't look like when it's happening.

So far so good, perhaps. But before we begin to look at what I think are the huge implications of seeing all love as having God as its source, and its only source, we'd better face up to a danger in this line of thought, as I mentioned earlier. Or in fact two closely related ones. The first is that we might run away with the idea that all manifestations of love are equally godlike, or that giving or receiving love can of itself bring us to God. C. S. Lewis is clear about this. He describes the qualities of what he calls 'our Gift-loves' – 'Their joy, their energy, their patience, their readiness to forgive, their desire for the good of the beloved' and comments that 'We may say, quite truly and in an intelligible sense, that those who love greatly are "near" to God'. But he warns that this 'is "nearness by likeness". It will not of itself produce "nearness of approach"'.[5] Clearly it would be ridiculous (and in bad taste, which is worse) to suggest for instance that the ecstasy of sexual love is the same as the love of God, and for God, that we hope to discover when we eat the bread and drink the wine of the Eucharist. And it would be stupid and indecent to suggest that the one could act as a substitute for the other, or that the one could lead seamlessly to the other. And yet, and yet, perhaps a greater danger in rightly seeking to avoid such lèse-majesté is of thinking that there is no correspondence between these loves at all, and that only one is worthy of being mentioned in the same breath as any talk of God.[6] And the same thing could be said of the appearances of love in other contexts. Somewhere, somehow, even if faintly, those 'other' loves can be traced back to God who is love. Marred they may be, by humanity's self-exclusion from

God's best way, but from God they are, nonetheless. Jesus was willing to talk to Peter about *philia* love, after all.

The second and related danger is that if all love has God as its source, we might think that we can move from saying 'God is love' to saying 'love is God'. Linguistically and philosophically this is the equivalent of the logic error that says 'all horses are creatures with four legs, therefore all creatures with four legs are horses'. We can't make the thought run backwards. Pantheism confuses the creation with the creator, and risks worshipping or at least revering the one instead of the other. We are called to worship the creator, and not the creation. But as long as we are sure to get that the right way round, we can be brave in how we look at the creation. It bears the marks of its creator's character, and we will see shortly that it does that to a greater extent than we may have realised. But creation it is, and it is not something that exists separately from the God who is love. So we should expect to find love written across the whole of creation. Finding that love and learning to identify it in perhaps surprising places will not of itself bring us to God – Lewis's 'nearness of approach'. For that we need God's revelation of himself as love in the face of Christ. But we can only begin to understand the breadth and length and height and depth of that love (Eph 3:18) if we develop the ability to see love wherever in the universe we might look.

As well as the danger of thinking that other loves have no common parentage with the love revealed as *agape*, there is a further snag that we need to be aware of. It's very easy for us to think that the *agape* love revealed in the coming and the actions of Jesus is some new aspect of the character of God. Well, new to us perhaps, but not new to him. This is an absolutely crucial point for what we may think of as our 'method' in this exploration of the meaning of love. Whatever we may say about him must be true, and must *have been* true, always. Whatever is in his nature must always have been so, even if different aspects of it are shown to us at different stages. Whatever we may learn about him and his character, from considering the creation, through the story of his self-disclosure to his chosen people, and finally his self-disclosure in Christ, must be true of him from eternity.

We are stretching the limits of language and thought here, and as I warned in the Preliminaries, we need to acknowledge the poverty of our attempts to speak about God in any definitive way. But with that caveat, we can say that although he seems to be primarily a God of action, and that action takes different forms according to the situation, what does not change is the nature from which those actions spring. If that were not so, we would not be able to rely on him. The multiple and capricious gods of the Greeks and the Romans must have been a nightmare to live with, and against their unpredictable behaviour the Christian God was presented as unchanging in his nature, though liable to surprise in his actions. It must have been a great relief to those who turned from the many to the One. And of course that 'faithfulness' was rooted for the first Christians in the revelation of God's nature that is in our Old Testament. So we can take our 'new' understanding of the love of God in Christ and take it with us as we rewind the film, just as scientists were able to do when they discovered that the universe was expanding. That discovery allowed them to think the thought that one could imaginatively reverse the process, and so they arrived at the mind-expanding idea that there must have been a beginning from which the expansion began – the Big Bang that we all know about with perhaps too easy familiarity. In just the same way we can – we must – take God's Jesus-revelation of his nature and allow it to inform the way we think about God as creator. Whatever he is like in the person of Christ, he must have been like that in his nature also when he created, and before he created. We are truly stretching language and thought. Arthur Peacocke puts it like this: 'Love and self-sacrifice are ... inherent in the divine nature and expressed in the whole process of creation.'[7] But we are getting ahead of ourselves, and must wait till a later chapter to develop some thoughts on how we might be able to speak of love in the context of speaking about the creation.

So for now, this rewinding back towards the creation will include all the rich understanding of the love of God which is housed in our Old Testament, the record of God's dealings with his covenant people. We would look in vain, of course, for any direct equivalent of *agape* in the Old Testament, if for no other reason than the obvious one of it being written in Hebrew. But perhaps there are glimmers, or much more, of the concept, if not of the word. It is the idea of God's faithfulness that we noticed a moment ago. The Hebrew *chesed* is variously translated as mercy, or unfailing love, or compassion, or, in older versions, the beautiful invented word 'loving-kindness'. In many cases it relates to the fact that God refused to give up on his unfaithful covenant people. Trevor Dennis gives a fine exposition of it in his book *Sarah Laughed*:

> It is often used in the Old Testament of relations between human beings, but it is also very commonly applied to God. It is hard to translate, and it is impossible to convey all its nuances in a word or phrase. It speaks of mercy, kindness, love, fidelity, a love that will persist in the midst of great danger, and in the face of great provocation and rejection. It is often translated as 'steadfast love', and when it is used of God it tells of his enduring commitment to his people more powerfully than any other word.[8]

The other Hebrew word that becomes 'love' in our translations is *ahab*, and there is a fascinating alignment of *chesed* and *ahab* in Deut 7:12-13. If the people keep his commandments, then God will 'maintain with you the covenant loyalty' (*chesed*). This is followed immediately by the reassurance that 'he will love you' (*ahab*). This has the general meaning of 'having affection' for someone. It can be used in the context of sexual love, but ranges much more widely than this. So, to take just a few examples, it is the word used when Isaac marries Rebekah: 'She became his wife, and he loved her' (Gen 24:67). And in a quite different setting, after God gives the Ten Commandments for the second time, he tells the people that they must 'love him' (Deut 10:12) and that they must 'also love the stranger' (Deut 10:19). All these different senses use the root of *ahab*. And it is this word that is the backbone of the two verses that Jesus quotes in his summary of the law in Mk 12:30-31. 'Love the LORD your God with all your heart' and so on (Deut 6:5) and 'Love your neighbour as yourself' (Lev 19:18). It will be no surprise that Mark translates these verses with *agape*.

In Deut 7:12-13 it is God who is the lover in both words. But in Deut 5:10 he shows 'steadfast love (*chesed*) to the thousandth generation of those who love (*ahab*) me'. There is great fluidity between the use of the two words, and it is clear that both can be applied to the actions of God and of his creatures. This is certainly a rich Old Testament soil from which the New Testament writers were able to cultivate their understanding and experience of *agape*. By then it had become clear that God's chosen people had found themselves unable to live up to their perhaps impossibly high calling. This was nothing less than to show the world what the one God of love was like, and how his creatures should reflect that love. Those who had lived and worked with Jesus, or were the immediate inheritors of their story, were beginning to realise that this aspiration had been lived out in front of their eyes, with all the implications for who that person might have been, and what that might mean for the community of his followers.

Of course it would be naïve to suggest that the Bible is only talking about love when it uses some words that we can translate in that way. The whole narrative of the Bible is about how God has let us know that the meaning of everything is love, so it is possible – and, as we shall see, imperative – to read any part of it as being underpinned by that truth. We will look at this in much more detail as we go along. But more specifically, the context of the love that the New Testament writers wrote about was entirely focused on the nature of the God revealed in Christ, and on the love response of the person and community that had found that love.

This love, though, is not divorced from other loves that we can know about, because, as we have seen, all love has God as its source. Humans are broken, certainly, and the contexts of our loving are complex, with the result that many of our loves will reflect their source only dimly at best, rather as the more distant planets shine less brightly than those nearer the burning sun. But there is no other sun from which the light of love can come. So it is legitimate to continue our enquiries by looking at human love in all its wonderful variety, in order to find some preliminary markers as to the nature of the universe that God has set up. God speaks to us in only one language, and we are wired up for it already.

Interruption I: Overtaken by Events?

This book has been a long time in the making. Towards the end of 2013 I began to make some preliminary notes for what I hoped might one day turn into a book on the supremacy of love. In particular I was beginning to wonder how I could characterise essential aspects of human love, and use them as a necessary staging-post in thinking more widely about a universe that might run on love. But on 8 Nov 2013, Typhoon Haiyan made landfall in the Philippines. It was probably the fiercest typhoon over land in recorded history. The damage and loss of life were huge and tragic. More than 6,300 people lost their lives in the Philippines, and many more in other areas of Southeast Asia. But once the immediate emergency aid had been given, and the event itself had passed out of the headlines, the ongoing needs of that country remained. Livelihoods to be restored, infrastructure to be rebuilt, and countless broken human lives to be repaired, if that is possible. Then only a few weeks later, there were heartbreaking pictures of Syrian refugees in Lebanon. Having escaped from the devastation of the civil war in their country with their lives but little else, their flimsy tents were covered in snow after the worst winter storm in Lebanon in decades. Two years later, the plight of refugees from Syria was more acute than ever. And more recently, in 2017, we have watched as hurricanes devastated parts of the Caribbean and southern United States, and as floods brought loss of life and destroyed homes and infrastructure in northern India, Nepal and Bangladesh. In such a world, is it not meaningless and (which is worse) indecent to talk airily of a universe ruled by love?

Almost all commentators agree that a single event cannot be directly identified as the result of climate change, but they agree also that climate change will increase the frequency and severity of extreme weather events. Typhoon Haiyan will not be the last.

There are of course a few, and scientists among them, who are adamant either that climate change is not happening, or that it is not human-induced. One might legitimately feel that they are today's equivalent of those who continued to believe that the earth was flat even when faced with the glorious evidence of the now iconic photo of Earthrise over the moon taken by the Apollo 8 astronauts on Christmas Eve 1968. The climate of earth has of course changed many times in the impossibly long history of its existence, long before there were any humans to mistreat it and reap the consequences. But if we go with the majority verdict (by far) and agree that climate change is happening and that for the first time humans have at least some, and probably major, responsibility for it, it is certainly the case that it is the poor, such as those in the Philippines, who will suffer more from its effects. There are at least two reasons for this.[1] First, because of geography: those living in areas more at risk tend to be poor, for instance because they live in low-lying areas which will be the first to feel the effects of a rise in sea levels, and which are therefore less desirable to live in, and so less expensive. Second, because poor countries have less resilient infrastructure that might enable them to mitigate the effects of climate change.

So there is human responsibility in the mixture of cause and consequence that we are now seeing. But let's be honest: some of the damage, which one could loosely identify as beginning with the industrial revolution, was done long before its consequences could be foreseen. Coal fired that revolution, and although industrialisation blighted the lives of the poor (again), it also enabled the growth of the kind of prosperity that we now take, rightly or wrongly, to be axiomatic for what humans should expect from life on this planet. It seems reasonable to conclude that there is a much greater weight of guilt, if that is not putting it too strongly, and I think it isn't, upon those of us who have been made aware of the consequences of our actions than upon those who acted in ignorance. We are truly reaping the whirlwind.

But however great may be our contribution to the present crisis of climate change, and we will return to this in due time, this was always going to be a world where disaster was available on the menu. Not all that's problematic about the world can be laid at the door of human sin, or sinfulness, which is the Bible's shorthand for the fracturedness of our lives, not fully connected to the One who is the source of everything. Mountains are formed and earthquakes and tsunamis triggered by the unimaginable force of tectonic plates grinding against each other; volcanoes erupt and throw carbon dioxide into the air, which at least in the early history of the earth was the means by which an atmosphere first came to surround it, providing the means for breathing life to develop; winds blow; trees grow and their leaves soak up some of the carbon dioxide in the atmosphere; seas rise and fall; rain waters the earth. There is no need to spell out the downsides of these life-giving aspects of our world. Without these things there would be no life, and nothing interesting would happen. We would certainly not be here to agonise over it. Through them we are brought into life and sustained. But through them also we may meet disaster and an untimely end. And if we avoid those, it is indirectly through them and as a consequence of the kind of active, dynamic world that they permit, that we shall surely die. We will return soon enough to thinking about how we should treat such a creation, and how we should live in it. But the question for now is more philosophical, or more theological perhaps: is it possible to speak in the same breath of a creation made out of love and of the uncomfortable fact that the creation is open to disaster?

Out of those two, the fact is incontrovertible. The reference to love is where the difficulty lies. Without in any way meaning this to be a kind of semantic conjuring trick, it may be the case that if there is a solution to the conundrum, it may lie in the detail of how we choose to define (or, better, as we saw a moment ago, recognise) and understand love. So the events that made me

19

stop and think as I was just beginning to put material together for some thoughts on human love may give us even more of a reason to see and perhaps redefine (by its actions) what this thing is that we call love. It may not be entirely what we thought.

Love Makes the World Go Round

To err is human; to forgive, divine.
(Alexander Pope)[1]

'Listening in'

One of the implications of Pope's perhaps too well-known aphorism might be that there is some kind of chasm between the nature of God and the nature of humans, and that what is true of God cannot be true of us.[2] Well of course in one sense that's true. The Bible has plenty to say about how 'we have all turned to our own way' (Is 53:6), and we can see that the whole narrative of the Bible is the record and explanation of what God has done about it. 'The LORD has laid on him the iniquity of us all', Isaiah continues. But in spite of the dimensions of the chasm, it is not the case that things have gone so wrong that God cannot make contact. After all, Christianity is revelation or it is nothing. God did not abandon his project, but made himself known, little by little. And if he was to do that, it must be in a language that we would be able to understand, or at least that we are capable of learning. It turns out that he has used the only language there is.

If God speaks in the language of love, and has made that the language of the universe, then it must be a language that we already know how to use, even if fallibly, otherwise his words to us in the language of love will be incomprehensible. Then, of course, he will teach us to become more fluent in his language, but that is an idea to keep for later in our discussion. So if all love has God as its source, it is legitimate to enquire into our human experience of love in order to learn something about God's love. This won't tell us all we need to know, but it will certainly tell us something. Human loves are faulty and fallible and full of contradictions, to be sure, but not to the extent that they have lost all connection with their creator. There is indeed a chasm, but God has reached across it, speaking the language of love. The path that connects the love of God to my daily life with its smaller loves is not a one-way street, but each reaches out to the other. Each makes sense of the other. And each is the goal of the other. Certainly, Christianity is revelation, not human invention. (We could note in passing that if it were the latter, we might expect it to tie up many more loose ends than seems to be the case.) But that revelation is spoken in our language, so there is two-way traffic. I find an echo of this in my work as an accompanist. The basic shape of a performance will be laid down over the countless hours of practice and rehearsal. But in the moment of performance, the way I hear a phrase being sung or played by my partner may suddenly shed light on my next phrase, making me perhaps deliver it in a slightly different way to what we had planned. And then of course that will be picked up by my partner and bring its own possibilities for response. In rather the same way, there is mutual responsiveness in the sharing of the language of love between God and his creatures.[3] If I develop my capacity for human love, I will, perhaps without knowing it, be developing the capacity to love God. And if I have glimpsed anything of the love of God, that must affect and inform the life of my daily loves.

Of the making of many books on the subject of love, there is no end. So the thoughts that follow do not claim to say something no one else has thought of. Rather, they are an attempt to pick out what we might think of as the basic rules of the grammar of this language, so that we can refine our ability to recognise it when it is being spoken, and begin to speak it better ourselves.

But before we can safely do this, we need to pause for a moment. This look at human love is legitimate, I have been suggesting, because 'God is love'. All love has him as its source, so we may find out something useful by learning about love in general, unwrapped from the religious packaging in which it's often presented in a Christian context. But what kind of statement are we making when we say 'God is love'? Well, for one thing we are directly quoting John in 1 Jn 4:8,16. The language is so simple that it's possible to overlook what kind of claim he is making. In an earlier chapter (I Jn 1:5) he says that 'God is light'. This sounds like a similar statement. But I want to suggest that it is in fact dissimilar, and in a very important way, which has huge implications for our investigation into love. This difference concerns metaphor.

In a previous book[4] I proposed the metaphor of God the Composer as a way of trying to understand something of his creative process in what is for us a very messy world. I was, I hope, careful to point out that a metaphor like that can only go so far. It certainly can't encompass all that needs to be said about God, and will illustrate and illuminate only a tiny corner of his nature and activity. Metaphors are useful, but limited. Vincent Brümmer points out that by concentrating on a way in which one thing is like another, which is what a metaphor is, we can fail to see that it is also saying something about ways in which the one thing is not like the other. Metaphors 'always contain the whisper, "it is *and it is not*"'.[5] So if we think about John's claim that 'God is light' we can see that he is using this idea to help us to sense God's holiness, and the fact that he can shine a light into the dark places of our lives and show them up in all their messiness, in order to heal them. (Of which the corollary is that if we claim to follow him, we had better 'walk in the light' (v 7) and aim to exhibit the family likeness.) But, this being a metaphor, there is an *'and it is not'*. He is not, for instance, saying that sometimes God goes out of sight over the horizon for a few hours; or, if he were writing today, he would not be saying that God must simultaneously be thought of as a wave and a particle (which is how light behaves according to the ever-mysterious quantum theory). God is, but also is not, light.

If we now return to John's simple but profound statement that God is love, what can we identify as the *'and it is not'* element of that metaphor? I asked myself that question, and a long silence followed in my head. I could come up with no satisfactory answer. And the reason for that is that it is not a metaphor at all. It is not a way of saying something which, although helpful, only takes us so far before it breaks down. To say that God is love is not a picture with limited applications. It is the thing itself. To put it straightforwardly: God is in some ways like light, and in other ways not; but he is not 'like' love in some ways but not in others. He *is* love. So John's two aphorisms, though superficially similar, are of quite different kinds, and the one about love expresses a depth of truth that takes it far beyond 'mere' metaphor, enlightening though such ideas can be. He is telling us abut the fundamental nature of the universe. That is why it's legitimate to look at any kind of love that we have experience of, and in so doing attempt to find out something about God. Later on we will try to see if what we can discover about human love can illuminate, or at least be compatible with, the idea of a God who creates in love. We will be asking what we might expect to see if indeed the universe is made of love. But to know what we are talking about, we must start with what we know of our own loves.

There are as many kinds of love as there are hearts.
(Tolstoy, *Anna Karenina*)

Tolstoy is right, and, as he implies, what links all these different kinds of love is that they take place within hearts. So is love a feeling? Certainly one would think so, to judge by most contemporary comment. The western postmodern world-view, which says that something is right if it feels right for me, would confirm this. But let's not be too harsh: to have been 'in love', with all the physical and yet more-than-physical aching that goes with it, is to have felt truly alive, in a way and with an intensity that no other experience can reproduce. Or as a musician, I have had the privilege of being caught up in the huge emotional power of a great piece of music, and of helping the audience to enter into it too. That too is a kind of love, shared between composer, performer and listener. But in both these cases, the feeling is the by-product, not the thing itself. The feeling may well assure us that the experience is real, but the love, of whatever sort, predates the feeling – if only by a microsecond.

We will return later to a fuller consideration of such feelings, but I want to start this brief look at human love in what is perhaps a surprising place, by thinking about things without which love cannot claim to be the real thing. They are not the thing itself, but are, if you like, its flavours. 'The taste of a lemon' is not the same as 'a lemon'; but if it doesn't taste of lemon, there's not much chance that it is one. As Tolstoy reminds us, there are an infinite number of ways in which we can love and be loved and observe love, so it would be an impossible task to quantify them all. But there are things which must be there if we are to call something love. As we have seen, there are many different and appropriate contexts for love. If I am lucky, I may love my job; I love the smell of a bonfire in autumn; I love my children and their children. But, leaving aside love for God and his for me, which we will come to eventually but not yet, such loves as these all happen within the context of whatever is my highest human love. For many, though not for all, that will be the love for another person with whom we wish to spend our lives. So the following thoughts will refer to this love, which is a marker for all our loves. Much of it, though not all, will apply also in the different contexts of other loves, but it seems sensible to come at this from the viewpoint of this love that can overwhelm us and change us as we enter into a life partnership. This is not at all to demean or devalue the experience of the many people for whom love of this kind doesn't happen – either through choice or in spite of a deep desire that it should. This is not at all about suggesting that there are different levels of human value. All are equally precious to God, and should be so to each of us who are made in his image. All are the equal objects of God's love, and all are able to respond to and reflect that love in his or her own circumstance of life. My own experience is of the privilege of having found a life partner, and so it is from that experience that I must write. [It is perhaps important to issue a 'spoiler alert' here. The following thoughts may seem so idealistic as to bear little relation to life as we tend to experience it. Perhaps. But I would ask the reader to stick with it for now, with the promise that we shall in due course be brought down to earth with a generous helping of reality.]

To the extent that we are perhaps inclined to think that love is fluffy and cuddly, this first, and most important, thing without which love cannot claim to be genuine may seem surprising. In this age where, at least in the West, personal happiness and fulfilment are seen as the things to strive for, it may seem curiously out of step with the life we are told to aspire to by advertisers, manufacturers, economic commentators and self-styled personal guides. **Love is costly**. It hurts, or at least it may do. If there is no chance that it could, then whatever else it may be, it isn't love. For evidence of this, we could, if we can bear it, think of the heartbreaking text messages sent by the students on board the stricken South Korean ferry which sank in April 2014, with the loss of many young lives. To watch the grief of waiting parents, whose children had sent them messages of love, felt intrusive, such was the personal agony they were enduring. One message said 'This may be the last chance I have to tell you that I love you'. Perhaps we need look no further for evidence that love is the meaning of the universe, and perhaps we can only truly see it from the perspective of the extremes of suffering and terror. For parents and children, love was indeed infinitely costly.

But is this cost only paid when something terrible is happening? Could there not be a love which, when all is going well, has no cost, but only gives, only adds to the sum of our happiness? Falling in love can certainly feel like that. The sky is a deeper blue, the song of the birds is fuller and more intense, and time itself conspires with our hearts to be the vehicle that brings the presence of the beloved to us. Poets have always understood this. Goethe was finely tuned to the intimate connection between the physical world and the condition of our hearts, which is one of the 'big ideas' of Romanticism:

> *Ich denke dein, wenn mir der Sonne Schimmer vom Meere strahlt,*
> *Ich denke dein, wenn sich des Mondes Flimmer in Quellen malt ...*
> I think of you when the sun's gleam streams back, reflected in the sea,
> I think of you when the moon's light is painted in the spring waters ...

But this beautiful poem ends in uncertainty and paradox:

> *Ich bin bei dir, du seist auch noch so ferne, du bist mir nah!*
> *Die Sonne sinkt, bald leuchten mir die Sterne, O wärst du da!*
> I am with you; though you are so far away, you are near me!
> The sun goes down, soon the stars will shine on me; if only you were here!

So whilst there can be rapture and delight, there is the possibility of absence and separation.

But perhaps all this is only a consequence of humanity's brokenness – what much biblical comment calls 'The Fall', though the Bible itself never uses that term. Perhaps in a world perfectly attuned to the presence of God, and aligned with his purposes and character, there could be love with no cost. All the joy and none of the pain. Perhaps there is only a cost to love because everything has gone horribly wrong. I suggest not, and this is an absolutely crucial thought for our exploration of love. In a later chapter we will see what these flavours of love can tell us about a God who may have created the universe out of love. But if the love that we experience as humans is in its fundamental nature mis-aligned with what it is like for God to love, then he will be speaking to us in a language whose meaning is lost to us, like some of the ancient hieroglyphs and other writing systems whose meanings can only be guessed at. On the other hand, if the possibility of cost and loss is inseparable from the content of love even for God, then the consequences for how we view his universe are huge.

Goethe in his poem shows that pain and cost may come because of physical separation from the object of our desire, and this seems a pretty basic fact of life. It's impossible to conceive of a world in which we could always be with the beloved. And it gets worse: to have love with no pain and no possibility of separation wrapped up in it, there would have to be a world in which we had never *been* separated. Taken to this extreme, it would be a world in which there was no 'falling in love' at all. We would be in a constant state of 'having fallen' in love, with no 'before' attached. This is the stuff of nightmares. There could be none of the glorious sensation of being overwhelmed by the new, and there could be none of the longing which aches for fulfilment. There could be no personal decision to love – we would be the immobile victims of our destiny. We might think we were loving, perhaps, but it could not be the real thing.

A further and more painful kind of separation is the separation that comes from rejection. I am in the presence of the beloved, but the beloved walks away. Love cannot be commanded. One of the main features of a psychopathic personality is a lack of empathy, and this is closely linked to behaviour in which the psychopath attempts to control the emotional interaction between him- or her-self and a victim. In the context of personal relationships, this may often take the form of trying to force the other into certain types of behaviour, as many an abused partner will testify. Those of us who are at least relatively healthy in our minds know that it is impossible for love to live in this environment. Vincent Brűmmer puts it like this: 'Mutual commitments can only be fulfilled in mutual freedom. Neither partner can coerce or oblige the other to remain faithful without thereby implicitly perverting the relationship into a manipulative one or into a contractual agreement.'[6] But this permission for the other to respond carries with it the equal and opposite permission not to do so. That is the potential cost of love. Without this cost, as Mr Spock never said in Star Trek, it 'might be love, Jim, but not as we know it'.

In parenthesis I wonder how this acceptance that the other's freedom is needed for love to flourish, with the possibility of rejection that this opens up, stands in relation to the growing habit of Hollywood celebrities and others to enter into 'pre-nuptial agreements'. The abbreviation 'pre-nup' is reason enough to think that this is an emaciated expression of the desire of two lovers to be together for ever – as unlovely linguistically as it is dispiriting conceptually. To be sure, no one can guarantee that a relationship will last 'till death us do part', but it seems to me that if at the beginning the talk is of how we'll carve up the estate if we fall out, then this is the death of idealism. At least the intention must be there otherwise we are not talking about love. We will have reduced the thing to a contract with perks, sexual or otherwise. Proper love risks everything on the most important wager of all – that this love will last and grow and change both of us for the better. Goethe's first novel, and the work that turned him into a celebrity across Europe, was *Die Leiden des jungen Werthers* – the sorrows of young Werther. With hindsight we might see that the eponymous hero's unrequited passion for an already-married young woman was never going to end well, and indeed he ends up committing suicide. In this respect he is perhaps more of an anti-hero. But at least he risked everything, rather than settling for a smaller life. Sadly, after the book was published, there was a spate of real-life suicides in emulation of our tortured protagonist. So whilst one cannot hold up the story as a guide to the wise life, at least the picture rings true of love as total commitment, come what may.

That total commitment will at some point also involve paying the cost of forgiveness. It is part of our human condition to fail to live up to whatever standards we have set for ourselves. Even if at some stage of our lives we are able to live out the privilege of a relationship of love where acceptance is chosen over rejection, and where the cost of physical separation has been repaid in the constant presence of the beloved, yet still we will spoil things for the one we love. There is no need to enumerate all the ways, large or small, in which we can behave in a way that requires forgiveness from the other. But if that forgiveness is sought and received, then the love that enabled the forgiveness will be validated and strengthened. We could rewrite Pope's aphorism, and say that if forgiveness is divine (and we will look later at the cost to God of that forgiving), then when we forgive, however temporarily and partially, we are just beginning to be remade into 'the image of God'.

We cannot leave this exploration of the cost of love without paying attention to another situation where the cost can be overwhelming, and in this case it is to be found in what the love between life partners may produce – the experience of being a parent. I referred earlier to the messages from the children on the South Korean ferry. For the parents, the cost of parenthood was infinite. But even in less traumatic circumstances, it is impossible to be a parent without paying a price. And the price comes at each moment, when, however imperceptibly, the child must grow away from the parent, in order to become a fully-formed adult. Even from the moment the baby leaves the security of the mother's body to which it has been utterly and wholly connected, through, one day, the baby's first turning of the head away from the mother, to the day when the child, no longer a child, leaves home for the first time. C. Day Lewis wrote heartbreakingly about this in his poem *Walking Away*.[7] He remembers the day eighteen years before, when a child was playing football for the first time, and imagines 'That hesitant figure, eddying away / Like a winged seed loosened from its parent stem'.

This turning towards one other person, with all the potential for gain and for loss, brings us to the next aspect of love, without which it cannot be said to be authentic. (It too contains a paradox, but we will leave that to one side for a moment.) The best illustration I know of this comes in an extraordinary moment in Schubert's song cycle *Die Schöne Müllerin*. Our hero this time is an itinerant manual labourer who gets work at the mill and has the misfortune to fall in love with the eponymous 'beautiful girl from the mill', who is, we are allowed to infer, the daughter of the mill-owner. In that world, such a relationship across the boundaries of class and privilege was doomed from the start. But in an early song, *Am Feierabend*, he berates himself for his inability to catch her attention – if only he had a thousand arms to turn the mill wheel himself, she would see how true was his love for her, but he can do no better than all the other mill-workers. Then, as they relax at the end of the day, the master thanks the labourers for their work, and the girl wishes them good night. Except it's not as simple as that. Schubert's genius is to take a fairly ordinary poem and fill it with the most painful psychological insight. In Wilhelm Müller's poem, she simply says '*Allen eine gute Nacht*' – Goodnight everyone. She only says it once, but Schubert repeats it, and inserts an accented chord before the second time, with a devastating change of just one note in the harmony. The German word order is 'to everyone, a good night'. So with the boy we hear her say it, and then with this devastating chord we hear that he has realised that she has not picked him out for special mention, and he hears her words again, but this time in his overwrought imagination. That one chord is the involuntary tightening of the stomach, the butterflies, the physical response to devastation. 'Everyone', not 'and specially you'. **Love demands exclusivity**.

Does this seem rather harsh as an indispensable flavour of love? Well, you could say we're in good company. In his elaboration of the Second Commandment, God says that the reason we must not make idols for ourselves is that 'I the LORD your God am a jealous God' (Ex 20:5). And there are plenty more references through the Old Testament to his jealousy for his people, who keep turning away from him and following other gods. He wants them for himself. To be sure, there is more to love than this, but the refusal to accept the claims of a rival is one mark at least of the real thing. If I claim to be in love with someone, and then show no particular sadness if someone else takes my place, then any onlooker would say that the love I professed was not genuine.

The paradox in this, which I mentioned earlier, is that this exclusivity is lived out in the context of all our social interactions. The intimate, intentional and exclusive connection to one other person does not mean that all other relationships are rendered invalid. On the contrary, this exclusive relationship can only work in a non-destructive way if it connects correctly to family, the immediate social circle, and wider society. In the Anglican wedding liturgy in its most recent form, there is a powerful and significant addition after the couple have said 'I will'. The congregation is asked whether they, the families and friends of the couple, will 'support and uphold them in their marriage, now and in the years to come', and they reply 'We will'. This correctly places the new relationship firmly in its immediate social context. By becoming part of someone else, I find the way to be part of society. We are in this together.

So there is a sense in which, by giving myself to someone else, I am giving myself also to a wider set of relationships. I become a small part of a much bigger picture. If I go up close to a picture by Monet, I can see a vast number of individual brush-strokes and tiny applications of paint, but the picture only makes sense if I move far enough away not to be able to see this level of detail. The specific recedes, and becomes part, and an essential part, of the whole. And now this idea of self-giving towards an exclusive relationship, yet which is lived out within society, brings us to an even greater paradox, and a fundamental one.

To love is to hold oneself back – but that leads to the enlargement of self. Perhaps love *is* the process of self-limiting? Or self-limiting *is* the activity of love? 'I'll have to ask my other half' we say, casually, and perhaps without realising that we are retelling a myth from Plato's *Symposium*. The story is that originally humans had four arms, four legs, two faces and so on. In order to prevent them becoming too powerful and threatening his authority, Zeus cut them in half down the middle. You might say he cut them down to size. And humans have ever since been looking for their other, perfect and complementary half. The one for, and perhaps from, whom they were made. Though falling in love may feel like this, it's not a picture that will lead to a healthy relationship. The danger is that, Narcissus-like, I am actually looking for the person most like myself that I can find. Online dating services offer the chance to 'Find your perfect partner', with the implication that that will be someone with the same attributes of character. The person who signs up 'wltm' (would like to meet) someone for instance with a 'gsoh' presumably because he or she thinks that a good sense of humour is a notable feature of their own identity. Then if later in the relationship they find that he or she is not as much like them as they expected, these differences may become a source of conflict, rather than of growth. A more healthy perspective is beautifully suggested by John Armstrong in his book *Conditions of Love*: 'The experience of learning to love someone in the long term involves various adaptations of oneself to the other; it involves dropping certain demands, learning others, changing priorities. But if you are able to do this with one person you would probably have been able to do it with another – at least with some others. Compatibility, on this view, is an achievement of love, not a precondition for love.'[8]

That achievement involves a change in oneself. I know without a doubt that after 47 years of marriage, I am, for better or worse, a different person than the innocent abroad who met his future wife in their first week at music college. To be sure, much of that change is due to external circumstance, and all the infinite number of events, large and small, that demand a response, and the infinite number of decisions, from the sublime to the trivial, that make up a lifetime. But all these imperceptible changes take place within the context that someone else has been involved in my life. Here is a dangerous idea, which I think it is neither a denial either of a romantic view of love, nor of the idea that, for a Christian, God has a hand in such life decisions: had the initial conditions been different, for instance if one of us had gained a place at a different music college, maybe I would have married someone else, and might still perhaps have had a happy relationship. This would be a transposition of the well-known 'butterfly effect' into the world of relationships. Questions that begin 'what would have happened if ..?' are usually unproductive and merely speculative, for the rather obvious reason that the suggested event didn't happen. But the point here is that had I married someone else – or not married at all – I would now be a different person. The holding back of oneself that is a necessary part of a relationship of love is the very thing that permits and enables change and growth.

Looking back in this way, the result of the infinite number of almost imperceptible changes that come from living a life in the presence of another is rather like the process by which a coral reef is built up. It's a living thing, but grows too slowly for a human to see. However, at any previous moment in that process, the next future detail was impossible to foresee, and this brings us to the next idea in our catalogue of things without which love cannot be said to be the real thing. **Love is experimental**. We cannot know how it will turn out.

My earlier book[9] had as its starting point some traumatic events that happened to our family. My subject then was concerned with trying to redefine what it might mean to be a Christian in a world where those events could happen. There was no need to go into any biographical detail about the stresses and strains that were visited upon the family, and upon the relationships of love within it, and there is no need to do so now. But certainly love was put under immense pressure by events that could not have been foreseen, and a way had to be found of respecting each individual's own pace and method of dealing with them. New ways of loving and of showing love were needed, and doubtless we all got it wrong at least as often as we got it right. But the point is that this all felt experimental, with very few guidelines other than the necessity for love to be looked for and practised and kept in view. John Armstrong writes wisely of 'a vision of love which sees problems not as the end of love, nor as a sign that love is over, but as the ground upon which love operates'.[10] This brings us back to our first idea, that love is costly. We cannot know how it will turn out. It may not turn out well. In particular, it may not be reciprocated. If I demand that the object of my love or desire do as I wish and answer love with love, and desire with desire, then I have not understood the first thing about the subject. To do this is to refuse the vulnerability that comes with any expression of love. It may be thrown back in my face, or merely be thought trivial and not worth responding to. The experiment that is love may fail. Or the experimental risk that accompanies love may be too much, leading to a kind of emotional paralysis, in which case love may be unable to declare itself, or take the next step. Thomas Hardy, with his acute sense of the passing of time, puts it with aching acuteness. He pictures a girl waiting in vain for her lover to come. He imagines her sad eyes: They ask, 'What indecision / Detains you, Love, from me?'[11] The inability or unwillingness to take the risk leads to a kind of blockage. She is waiting, but he will not or cannot make the move. The risk of the experiment is refused, and the opportunity passes, perhaps.

And that brings us to the final characteristic of love that we might identify as demonstrating its authenticity. In fact it incorporates two ideas, and we need to look at them simultaneously. **Love is purposeful, and is about relationship**. 'Love is not love / Which alters when it alteration finds, / Or bends with the remover to remove' wrote Shakespeare famously in his Sonnet 116. There is intention here. Once love has been awakened, the lover decides to direct that love outwards towards its object, and to stick with it regardless of circumstance. The familiarity of this truism can blind us to its significance: love cannot exist without an object, and it cannot exist outside the orbit of a relationship. Its purposeful goal is the growth of that relationship. I was going to say that if we are to go where love leads, there must be an intentional setting out, but I think that is only half right. The setting out must indeed happen, but we are not led by a feeling to a predetermined destination. Rather, the act of setting out unlocks possibilities. To be sure, the experience of falling in love feels anything but purposeful – much more like being swept along by something entirely exterior and uncontrollable. But we all know that this doesn't last – if it did, few of us would get much done! To keep the fire burning, once it has been lit, we have to decide that we will not alter or bend, but direct our intentions towards the beloved. And there we meet the perhaps obvious truth that love is directed towards another being – it cannot exist by itself, but must be in relationship with its object. That's where Narcissus went wrong. I cannot love without forgetting myself, and yet the wonderful paradox is that in so doing I discover who I am and what I am for.

The myth of Narcissus, who refused to be loved and then fell in love with his own reflection, tells us that to direct our love inwards instead of outwards leads to disaster. But what then are we to make of Jesus' words to the rich young man in Matt 19:19, quoting, as we saw in Chapter 1, Lev 19:18: 'You shall love your neighbour as yourself'? This is difficult to unpick, particularly as the verb uses the root of *agape*. How might love of self avoid the Narcissus Disaster? The question could be, and doubtless is, the subject of more than one long book, and we can only glance at it here. The command can certainly be glossed as 'love your neighbour as you would wish your neighbour to love you', but this seems to reduce its impact. Perhaps a starter thought might be that if God views me as worthy of his love, then that is how I should view myself. However, and by contrast, much Christian comment would tend to say, or at least imply, that I am not worthy of God's love, but for some reason he loves me anyway. This is how 'grace' is often portrayed. It finds horrifying expression in a hymn allegedly written for children. The first line 'I'm special because God has loved me' is a promising enough start, but after saying that Jesus was 'crucified to take the blame for all the bad things I have done', the killer line is 'I know I don't deserve anything'. This is psychological and emotional abuse dressed up, but not disguised, as a child-friendly introduction to the love of God. It is not at all redeemed by the closing line 'help me ... to know deep in my heart that I'm your special friend'. No: if God loves me, then it's because he can see in me, despite my flaws, something that awakens love in him.

Finally, in thinking about relationship, we need to notice that, of course, it is a two-way street. I wish to develop my connection to the other, but the vice versa must also be true if the relationship is to grow and flourish. So to be in relationship demands not just the desire to know, but the corresponding willingness to be known.[12] And that is perhaps the most dangerous and unsettling aspect of love. I am inviting the other person to see me as I really am. 'Naked, and ... not ashamed' is how Adam and Eve are described at the end of the second chapter of Genesis. This is not a re-imagining of some now-lost earthly paradise, for it's clear that such a thing never existed, but a deep myth about the human condition.[13] This is how we should be – open to the gaze of the other, and willing to be seen and known. Tragically, as the story continues, we find that too scary, and make coverings for ourselves, so that we cannot be fully seen by others, and, which is worse, we hope not to be fully seen by God. But we have not completely lost the desire and the ability to allow ourselves to be known. The awakening of love awakens that desire and willingness, and because of love we are able, however falteringly, to permit the terror of being known.

To complete the picture of life on this two-way street, a final unsettling aspect comes to mind. Just as I must be willing to be known, I must also allow the other person to satisfy my needs and desires. This is what the ancient philosophers meant by 'eros' – it's not so much about me satisfying my desires through the other, but more a case of me permitting the other to be the one who does this. And that satisfying is about more than sexual fulfilment, though it includes that of course. Why did I suggest that this is unsettling? Well, it seems to me that this is about renouncing power. I am allowing my lover to have the power to satisfy me, and this can only happen if I make myself vulnerable by acknowledging that I have the need to be satisfied. As I suggested earlier, in thinking about the mutual responsiveness between God and ourselves in speaking the language of love, there is a beautiful parallel here with the act of making music with someone else. A singer or violinist for instance may perform a particular phrase in a way that I hadn't thought of, and, if I am responsive, that will enable me to imitate it, or develop it or run with it as I play my own part, as the context requires. But I can only receive that gift if I have already made myself vulnerable by being prepared to be inspired in this way by the other person. As with music, then, so with love. To receive what I need, I have to face up to the fact that I am a lesser thing without the satisfaction that only the other can supply. For 'satisfaction' I originally wrote 'completion'. But that might imply that this process can come to an end. The glory of love is that there is always more to be given and received.

This chapter has been about looking for clues in our experience of love that might inform us when we try to say something about the love of God. We shall explore those possible connections in detail in Chapter 4, but for now, as a taster, here is a dangerous thought: can we dare to suggest that God falls in love with us (and, we may need to ask, with all of his creation)? If so, then this is a radically different picture of his love than the one we have been used to. That love often seems to be more of a generalised quality, in which we happen to get caught up. But we saw earlier that love only exists when it is active. Do we have to have a God to whom nothing ever really 'happens', with his love being no more than a generalised intention towards us? The interplay between his love and mine can feel unbalanced, with my response being personal, but his prior love that awakens mine being less so. Does his love have to be so radically different from what ours feels like? I fell in love with the woman who has been my wife these many years. Then I fell in love with my children. The way that later love was expressed and acted out was quite different of course, but falling in love it was. And now all over again with my children's children. I feel an overwhelming obligation to love them, but at the same time it feels entirely natural. I feel free in not being able to do otherwise. (Though of course I need to learn to do it better.) Why should God not do the same? But that puts it the wrong way round. This falling in love is part of what it means to be made in the image of God. It is possible for this to happen to us because it's what happens to God. He can fall in love.

But this raises an immediate problem: is God the passive victim of his own character? Can he not help being what he is and doing what he does? If that is the case, then suddenly it doesn't feel as personal and active and spontaneous as we might momentarily have dared to believe. This will need further investigation, which we will come to in due course, but for now, and briefly, yet another paradox might help. On the (perhaps rare) occasions when I feel, however dimly, that I am acting in line with those aspects of my character that are what God intends for me and wants from me, do I feel less free, or more? The glory is that even though this is not at any exalted level, and won't be at any exalted level any time soon, this feels like freedom, and not like being the prisoner of my character. When I act against God's intentions of character for me, then I feel less free. I see no reason why we should not be able to say the same about God. The difference is that he always acts in accordance with his (perfect) character, and so is always free. That is why we can speak of his *chesed*, his reliable and trustworthy character. This leads to another dangerous thought: perhaps, just perhaps, it may turn out that God needs us for his own satisfaction – and for his own infinite completion.

Cost and the possibility (and in some circumstances the necessity) of separation; exclusivity within a social context; a holding back that leads to self-enlargement; experiment and the possibility of failure; purpose, relationship and a willingness to be known; the vulnerability of allowing another to satisfy me. If those aren't there, it's not love.

Interruption II: Too Much to Ask?

O Love! They wrong thee much
that say thy sweet is bitter,
When thy rich fruit is such
as nothing can be sweeter
(Anon)[1]

In the previous chapter I referred briefly to some of the bitter stresses and strains visited upon my family by external traumatic events. But apart from that digression, you might well object that the description of those essential elements without which love cannot be said to be authentic was too idealistic by half, too much inclined to see love's fruit as rich and sweet, as these anonymous lines of poetry suggest. Perhaps, though, love's sweet is indeed bitter. Things generally don't go well. Love is offered and rejected; love flourishes and then withers under the strain of daily life and its slow accretion of snags, like an artery shaping up for a coronary; love is just too difficult or uncertain to embark upon, so it's safer to hide; love fails to survive the transition from skipping delight to plodding routine; for some, love just never happens.

One could argue that it's indecent to claim that the world and the universe run on the fuel of love. Or perhaps it's just naïve, which is probably worse. As I write this chapter, the news is still full of the seemingly endless civil war in Syria, with privileged countries being asked to take at least some of the millions of displaced and traumatised refugees, and Europe failing to know how to respond. War and instability in other Middle Eastern countries and in North Africa is fuelling yet more forced migration, and there are outbreaks of disease, particularly cholera, that are the direct result of conflict. The UN has characterised the violence meted out to the Rohingya people of

Rakhine state in Myanmar as ethnic cleansing, and Bangladesh, already poor, is overwhelmed with the influx of traumatised refugees. Not long before, the outbreak of Ebola in West Africa was claiming more lives. Although a 'natural' disaster of the kind we looked at in Interruption I, it was made disastrously worse by a lethal combination of undeveloped health services in countries that have the potential to be wealthy, of the overlay of cultural practices that make it almost impossible for populations to behave in ways that would limit the spread of the virus, and of a weight of corruption that stifles the best-laid plans. The earlier self-imposed Interruption was asking whether one could speak of love in a world in which natural disaster happens – and must happen for life to thrive, painfully paradoxical though that thought is. The problem before us for a moment now is rather different: all the evidence of human behaviour, failure and even our best-intentioned better moments seems to point in the other direction. A world in which 132 children and some adults can be murdered by the Taliban in a school in Peshawar, Pakistan, (December 2014) doesn't look like a world where love reigns.[2] A world in which journalists can be murdered in their office in Paris, and Jews in a shop the next day (January 2015) doesn't look like a world where love is doing very well. Or one could add the murder of all his passengers by a suicidal commercial pilot (March 2015), or the massacre of 148 people (April 2015), mostly Christians, at Garissa University, Northern Kenya, or the horrific violence perpetrated by the so-called IS, brought with shocking suddenness to the West in the atrocities in Paris (November 2015) and Nice (July 2016) or the bombing of hospitals and targeting of aid workers and supplies in Syria. Or the inexorable roll-call of terrorist outrages carried out, or claimed, by the same group as it lost territory in the Middle East. Or the death of 71 people in the probably avoidable Grenfell Tower fire in London in June 2017, which exposed the huge inequalities between the fortunate and the disadvantaged in one of the richest cities on earth. Or the decision of one man to open fire on a crowd of concert-goers in Las Vegas, in October 2017, with the loss of 59 lives and many others forever changed. Or the murder in November of the same year of 300 worshippers at a mosque in Egypt's North Sinai province. Or, I must add, the small and sometimes private but nonetheless real violations of the peaceable life in my own behaviour. The list could go on, and love is conspicuous by its absence.

The conventional, and I would add casual, Christian response often goes something like this: the world is a mess, but God has come to put things right – one conversion at a time. (Except, one might add, there's plenty of unloveliness in Christian settings – and I am part of it. Even Paul said 'I do the very thing I hate' (Rom 7:15)). This over-personalised picture is too thin to bear the weight of our instinctive longing for things to be better. To be sure, the process must start, as the saying goes, with me. I need to be changed, but so also does the way the world is run. Eyebrows were raised when Christian Aid began its campaign to challenge the unjust structures of society that lead to poverty and hunger. Their mission statement has been 'We fight injustice and inequality with courage, hope and determination, challenging the structures and systems that prevent people from rising out of poverty'. Those who might object presumably think God is only interested in the salvation of individual souls, and perhaps have not read the Old Testament prophets with their often savage denunciation of institutionalised injustice. But the process of putting things right seems so agonisingly slow that often it's impossible to see any progress at all. For this reason it's easy for Christian thought to slip into 'it'll be alright in the next life' mode. This will not do. It even leads some, particularly on the religious right in the US, to relish the prospect of future global trauma, whether through war or social or environmental disaster, as a way of hastening the coming glory. To be sure, there is no warrant in Christianity – and precious little evidence in these early years of the millennium – for the concept of the perfectibility of the human species,[3] and we are indeed encouraged to look forward to the time when God 'will wipe away every tear' (Rev 7:17; 21:4). But the urgent question is: what are we to make of now? Is there any evidence at all that the universe runs on love, and if there is, does it make any difference to today?

The rest of this book will, I hope, make the case that, if we can teach ourselves how and where to look, there is indeed evidence for the claim. But what we can't do is set up some well-intentioned balance-sheet exercise, where I point to examples of good stuff, and you point to examples of bad stuff, (or vice versa) and we see which weighs more. There is plenty of evidence for the good stuff. Just the day before the Pakistan school massacre, a gunman took hostages in a café in Sydney. Most of them escaped when armed police stormed the building, though many had serious injuries, but it was reported that the two who lost their lives had been attempting to protect the others. They gave up their own lives out of love. And every latest account of a terrorist attack or other act of violence is accompanied by reports of those who acted selflessly in order to help and protect others. But, as I have briefly sketched in this chapter, there is plenty for which the term 'bad stuff' fails to acknowledge sufficiently its distance in intention and result from the loving purposes of God. The point is not whether the good is doing better than the bad, or vice versa, but whether behind all the agony, or perhaps even within it, and in spite of it, love might be waiting, hoping, lurking with intent.

How then are we to learn to see evidence for love as the stuff of the universe in the midst of evidence to the contrary? An example or two from the varied worlds of science and musical performance may give us a pointer as to a possible method. There is an interesting phenomenon associated with the mechanics of the eye, and of some importance to those who enjoy amateur astronomy: particularly when light levels are low, as they of course are when we are looking at the night sky, one can see better by looking just to the side of the star or fuzzy nebula or whatever glorious celestial body it is, rather than looking directly at it. If we look the thing straight in the eye, it seems to disappear. For very different reasons, a rather similar thing can be the case for a musician. It's possible for a listener to assume that the 'inspired' musician is caught up in the emotion of the performance to a point where conscious thought is not required. Surprisingly, perhaps, this is not at all the case. The performer must of course be wholly engaged with the emotional content of the music – but this can only be achieved if conscious thought is directed towards the mechanics of playing the instrument at that moment. Charlie Chaplin is said to have remarked that the performer must be two people – the one going through all the emotions, and also the one organising the movements and gestures and so on. But there's a 'but', which is one reason why performing is so demanding. If this necessary conscious thought becomes *too* conscious, it can inhibit the natural movements that lead to the playing in public of the right notes in the right way, which have been built up over all those long hours of practice in private. The kind of consciousness required is more to do with recreating the sensations that have come to be associated with 'getting it right', and not so much to do with solving a technical problem all over again. If I focus too much on problem-solving at the moment of performance, this may inhibit the natural flow of technique, and therefore of musical expression. I almost need to trick myself into thinking of something else, (to do with the music of course!) in order for the hoped-for music to appear. This is the performer's equivalent of not looking directly at the distant star.

I think it may be useful to do something similar to these perhaps counter-intuitive techniques as we search for a way of learning to recognise love. To begin with, at least, it may be fruitful to take a sideways look at the thing we are hoping to find, rather than looking directly at it. To change the metaphor (and to use it in a happier context than the search for weapons of mass destruction which first brought the phrase into common parlance), we are looking for the smoking gun. We will be hoping to say in different contexts 'This may not be love itself, but it might be what we would expect to see if love were behind it'. So the next chapter will look at examples from music, science and literature, which, whilst not pointing directly to love itself, might yet be the kinds of things we could expect to see if the universe were indeed speaking the language of love.

3

Where in the World?

The world is charged with the grandeur of God.
(Gerard Manley Hopkins)[1]

'They're playing our tune'

Gustav Mahler finished his *Third Symphony* in 1896 – the longest symphony in the standard repertoire. As a young schoolboy I had the privilege of taking part in a number of performances, (though only as a member of the offstage boys' choir) before it was so widely known as it is now in the UK. It was one of the formative musical experiences of my short life up to that point. Without quite knowing it, I got a taste for the gigantic power of music, not just to engage the attention and emotions of an audience, but to say something about what it is to be alive, in a way that nothing else can do. Mahler originally gave titles to the six movements of this huge work, though he dropped them when the work was published in 1898. The final movement, which lasts almost half an hour, was called *'Was mir die Liebe erzählt'* – 'What Love tells me'. It moves slowly, with a gloriously rich harmonic language, for long passages using just the strings, but allowing itself a few passages of greater passion and energy. The movement, and therefore the whole gigantic symphony, finishes with a glowing, almost endless, D major chord, punctuated by triumphant, ecstatic strikes of the timpani.

Music is vital to our health precisely because it expresses things that can't be expressed in any other way. You might even say that we wouldn't know those things were there unless music brought them to our attention. In other words music doesn't itself create the feelings that it gives voice to, but allows them to come into view from deep down in our hearts onto the conscious, active surface of our being. The feelings, the ideas, the impulses, were there all along, but needed music to breathe life into them. If that is true, then rather than Mahler's glorious movement creating something that didn't exist before, it feels more as if it is expressing something we perhaps didn't know we knew until we heard it. Even though Mahler dropped the titles, they were clearly in his mind as he was writing, and the idea of the title seems entirely and miraculously appropriate to the music he wrote. So the experience and instinctive understanding of love that inspired Mahler predates the writing of the music. It is music's gift to unearth the love, to make it audible.

That's all very well – but most music isn't called 'What Love tells me'. So have I chosen a unique case whose significance can't be transferred to the rest of music? (And there's plenty of it.) Well I think not. I have argued elsewhere[2] that music (at least music that doesn't use words) is not really 'about' anything, and that it can't be pressed into the service of, for instance, a political ideal, without becoming a lesser and rather tawdry thing. Karen Armstrong puts it like this:

> Music goes beyond the reach of words: it is not *about* anything. A late Beethoven quartet does not represent sorrow but elicits it in hearer and player alike; and yet it is emphatically not a sad experience. Like tragedy, it brings intense pleasure and insight. We seem to experience sadness in a way that transcends ego, because this is not *my* sadness but sorrow itself. In music therefore, subjective and objective become one.[3]

I was going to say that music is simply about itself, but on reflection I don't think that's quite right. As we have seen, it facilitates – though that makes the process sound rather mechanistic – the coming into the open of feelings and ideas that can't be brought into the open by any other means. In other words, we know it not by defining its content, but by seeing what it does. And that is exactly what we discovered, in Chapter 1, about love itself. That is not at all to say that music is the same as love, but to say that music can awaken something very close to love, and which shares some of its characteristics.

Luke Bell gives us a helpful guide at this point, in a book subtitled *Recovering a Contemplative Spirit*. He speaks of 'the cosmos as a symbol rather than a machine, nature as meaningful rather than ripe for exploitation and a presence to be approached with love rather than fear ... the cosmos embodies the odyssey of the soul – it is all significant'.[4] In that spirit then: if music, and other arts, are one of the results of us being made 'in the image of God', who created in love, then what might we expect to see?[5]

No two performances of the same piece are identical. The written score, which seems so specific, is much less prescriptive than one might have thought. Tempo, balance between instruments, acoustics, the mood of the moment, the way the previous phrase just happened to go, and a thousand other indefinable variants – all these combine to ensure that 'this' performance is like no other. And before all that happens, the composer has had to choose constantly between an infinite set of possibilities. Neither composer not performer really knows how the piece and the performance will turn out. Our creativity is, by definition, experimental. Perhaps, if the universe runs on love, we should not be surprised.

The process of bringing the music into existence, and then of performing it – for it can hardly be said to exist in any meaningful way until it is performed – requires the attentive discipline of composer and performer, and of audience too. As a performer I can't just play a piece any way I like, even if I think I might like the result. The composer's wishes must take precedence over mine. But the paradox holds true, that if I accept this, and try to understand through the lens of my own personality why the composer wrote what he (or she) did, I will enlarge my capacity to blend my sensibilities with those of the composer. So I will grow as a musician by the very act of limiting myself, or holding myself back. And of course, before this could happen, the composer was in a similar way submitting to the prior demands of how music needs to be organised. Putting the sounds together into a piece of music is not at all arbitrary. Rather, the music seems to demand the right to exist, in a way that is prior to the composer's attempts to articulate it. And when all that is done, the audience enters into a pact with composer and performer. At least in the field of classical music, you don't shout out in the middle, even if you are enjoying it. You restrain yourself, in order to experience what composer and performer are offering from the deepest places of their hearts. By submitting, willingly, to this discipline, which in many ways is a holding back of the self for the sake of something greater, the individual and society are enlarged. And there is healing in it. The conductor Sir Simon Rattle said in a television documentary: 'Music says "you are not alone".' Though the detailed reactions to a piece of music will differ between all its hearers, nevertheless what it expresses is universal, and because of that it is able to unite those who hear it. Here is an echo of another of the flavours of love from Chapter 2: 'Perhaps love *is* the process of self-limiting? Or self-limiting is the activity of love.' Music isn't love, but if love runs the universe, then this may be how you might expect music to behave.

I mentioned a moment ago that music is there to be performed. I take this to be a given truth, not needing to be defended, which I came to believe strongly when I was a student reading Music at Oxford in the late 1960s. I reacted with some vehemence to what I felt was the prevailing view amongst some of those teaching the course, and certainly of those who set its exams – namely that it was sufficient to study music in a library, and that learning music was primarily an intellectual pursuit. A true musician will indeed want to know, and to understand; but these are a necessary means to an end, and not an end in themselves. Music is powerful and vital to our health precisely because, through the application of technique and intellectual understanding, it transcends these and expresses what cannot be grasped by intellect alone. In this way too it is not unlike love, which though open to reason and investigation, ultimately is what it is, and does what it does. As with music, so with love: there is no substitute.

Music behaves in the ways that we have seen. But it's perhaps important to point out, as I frequently do to my students, that it exists in the real world and not in some bubble where there are different rules that have no connection to other aspects of life. So music uses the normal physical properties of sound, and is created by the physical means of an instrument or voice. It takes hold of the passage of time, and is received via human ears into human consciousness, which, however mysteriously, resides in human bodies. So following on from these thoughts about the very physical business of making music, we can as it were go back a stage, and ask: how does the matter that fills the universe behave?[6] Can it give us any clues as we try to see whether on the evidence it is justifiable to view the creation as governed by love? The French mathematician and polymath Henri Poincaré (1854–1912) said this:

> The scientist does not study nature because it is useful; he studies it because he delights in it, and he delights in it because it is beautiful. If nature were not beautiful, it would not be worth knowing, and if nature were not worth knowing, life would not be worth living. Of course I do not here speak of that beauty that strikes the senses, the beauty of qualities and appearances; not that I undervalue such beauty, far from it, but it has nothing to do with science; I mean that profounder beauty which comes from the harmonious order of the parts, and which a pure intelligence can grasp.

His point is, I think, that there is a coherence to the way the world works, and that this points beyond itself to what he sees as beauty. It's interesting though, and rather paradoxical, that his work in mathematics and theoretical physics helped lay some of the foundations for the discoveries of quantum theory,[7] including the so-called chaos theory, and for Einstein's work on relativity. Paradoxical, because in the weird and wonderful world of quantum theory, 'harmonious order' isn't, at least at first glance, what we seem to be presented with. But maybe we can after all glimpse something coherent, and something that might, in its own language and according to its own lights, reflect and point to the kind of world we might expect to see if it ran on love.

Before we can start, though, this section must be accompanied by not one but two health warnings, one about science and what it can and cannot do, while the other is about who can or cannot talk about it. The first is the danger of the blurring of boundaries. Science is about making sense of the physical (though much more than just the visible) world. It asks 'what are the processes behind an observation?' and 'can those processes be codified into a theory?' Most scientists will justifiably rail at the teaching in the US of Intelligent Design as a supposed branch of science, and indeed a court ruling in 2005 took the view that it was sufficiently linked to the religious concept of creationism that to teach it as science violated the First Amendment, the separation between church and state. Science is about science, and cannot be press-ganged into doing what it's not for. Its abilities are huge, but also limited. It may be able to tell me a very great deal, and indeed it can, about how the universe works. But it is beyond its boundaries to say anything about a God who may have set the universe up in this way. But it might be reasonable to look and see if some of the things science can point to might be the sorts of things that look as if they could be consistent with a universe that had been set up to run on love.

The second danger, if this is not too perplexing, is the opposite one of the need for specialisation. It is a relatively modern idea that different areas of expertise should not overlap. To be sure, in one lifetime there's not usually time to excel in more than one field. The attempt to be a professional pianist and to practise that art has taken up most of my life. The hours of practice required put paid to much specialisation in any other area. But that is not the same as saying that these other areas have no contact with my area of expertise. It's more a question of practicality and the number of hours in the day, as well of course of the issue of what anyone is or isn't talented at. I have no idea *how* scientists do their experiments and come up with their theories, based on their observations. But I think we all have the right to rejoice in the amazing things they find, whatever our own area of skill. You could say that it comes down to what we mean when we use the word 'truth'. Pilate didn't wait around for an answer to that one, and perhaps should have done. I could say 'It is taking me a long time to write this paragraph' and then 'I ought to write it as well as I can'. One statement is science, an observed fact, while the other lives in the world of ethics. But the world only makes sense if both are sheltering under a large umbrella called 'truth'. So this (probably short!) section on science is being written by a professional musician, with all the opportunities for crass over-simplification or blatant misunderstanding and wrong-headedness that this opens up. But I think it's allowable to try, at least, to understand some of the conclusions of recent science (though they are always and only provisional) even if the maths and detailed knowledge that produced them are beyond any but the highly trained and scientifically literate. So here goes.

For the following thoughts I am indebted to that brilliant teacher Professor Brian Cox, who has a great gift for conveying the wonder of science to those with a desire to expand their horizons but who do not have formal training. And in particular a lecture he delivered in the famous lecture theatre of the Royal

Institution in London. It was called 'A Night with the Stars' and concerned the glories of the mind-baffling quantum theory.[8] Some of what follows are my own attempts to express the almost-inexpressible in terms that I as a layman can grasp, and I hope I have not made too many errors.

Brian Cox's main visual aid was a huge diamond. Being a diamond, it was made up of carbon atoms bound to each other in a particularly strong way. Each atom is made up of a nucleus, with electrons positioned around it. These electrons are arranged in positions of distance from the nucleus, in order of their energy, with the lowest energy 'closest in'. (This might give a wrong impression of everything being very close together. But paradoxically, at the level of the unimaginably small, most stuff is empty space.) We were then introduced to the Exclusion Principle discovered by Wolfgang Pauli in 1925, and elaborated in 1940. This states that two identical electrons cannot be at precisely the same energy level (or, more specifically, cannot occupy the same quantum state). To put it another way, the electrons in the diamond can't all inhabit the lowest energy level, so they have to find somewhere else to live. There are two consequences. The first is that all this allows chemistry to happen. The second, more important for our purposes, is that the Exclusion Principle applies to every electron in the universe, and that because they want (so to speak) to inhabit different places they must all be in communication with each other in order to achieve that. Brian Cox then heated the diamond by rubbing it between his hands. This put in energy, which resulted in the electrons being taken to different energy levels. Without needing to understand the maths, it's not difficult to see where this is going. As the heating takes place, every electron around every nucleus in the universe must be shifting to take account of it. This was summed up in the phrase 'Everything is connected to everything else'.

In a further thought experiment, the diamond was put in a box. The atoms in the box are always exploring every available path across the universe, so it's possible that when the box is opened, the diamond won't be there. By using a formula developed by Richard Feynman, which itself makes use of Planck's Constant, it is possible to work out the chance of this being the case when the box is opened. Because Planck's Constant is exceedingly small, it turns out that in this case, to have a reasonable chance of the diamond having disappeared, you would have to wait for 600 billion times the current age of the universe. This is reassuring, to say the least. Of course, the demonstration and the thought experiment were simply a way of showing by one example something that is happening at all times and in all places throughout the universe. So we have a mental picture of the whole universe working together, everything influencing everything else, a kind of resonance uniting a cosmos vaster and more mysterious than we can imagine. Now we need to be careful: some of what I have written might seem to imply some kind of consciousness or purposefulness to 'inanimate' matter. This is of course not how it is. Stuff just does what stuff does. But we have to find a language to express all this, which seems to call for some use of metaphor. So, with that caveat, and acknowledging that we have reached the edge, not of what science can discover of course, but of the kind of things it is allowed to tell us, is there anything in this amazing quantum world that we could see as running parallel with our search for evidence of what a love universe might look like?

Just this, I think: though we must use the word advisedly, there seems to be a sense of relationship amongst the very smallest things that give rise to the world as we experience it. This is relationship only on the electrons' own terms of course, and not in any way of the kind that is experienced by the higher creatures (probably) and by humans (certainly). But perhaps, just perhaps, if the universe means love, then it may not be surprising to find that electron can call to electron across the infinite reaches of space. Quantum theory says that the more certainly we know a particle's position, the less certainly we can know its momentum, and vice versa. This feels like a very experimental way of organising matter. With all this intimate relationship between particles, and the sense that they are in a constant state of being experimental, quantum theory gives us a glimpse into a world that is beyond strange, to be sure, but that we might be able to see as the possible work of a God who meant everything to be love.

It's the gift of a poet to be able through intuition to tell us what we might otherwise have missed. Shelley (1792–1822) wrote a beautiful poem called *Love's Philosophy*.[9] Long before quantum theory was even a glimmer in any scientist's eye, he jumped to an idea that expresses something of the same picture, transposed into human experience. 'Nothing in the world is single; / All things by a law divine / in another's being mingle –/ Why not I with thine?' Perhaps when we long for relationship with another, we are running with the grain of the universe. The German language (not Greek this time) has a word for it: *Sehnsucht*. This has more content than the dictionary translation of 'longing' might suggest in English. In keeping with Romantic sensibilities, it is often associated with being distanced from the homeland, and the longing for acceptance and belonging that separation produces. But in a sense this is only an illustration of a deeper longing, the desire to be united with another human being. And yet contained within this is the painful awareness that it can never be fully achieved. *Der Wanderer*, a wonderful song by Schubert, expresses this vividly in words by the splendidly named Georg Philipp Schmidt von Lübeck:

> *Wo bist du, mein geliebtes Land? Gesucht, geahnt, und nie gekannt!*
> *Das Land, das Land so hoffnungsgrün, das Land, wo meine Rosen*
> *blühn ...*
> Where are you, my beloved land? Sought for, felt for, and

never known!
The land so green with hope, where my roses bloom ...

But the poem ends with the devastating:

Dort, wo du nicht bist, dort ist das Glück!
The place where you are not, is where happiness is to be found!

This is *Weltschmerz* – another untranslatable German word meaning something like the pain associated with the world being the way it is. Now the conventional Christian response to this is on the one hand, as we noted earlier, that the pain is because we have chosen to walk away from God's best intentions for us, and on the other that everything will be put right in the next life. The first of these is unambiguous, and indeed is the backdrop for the whole Christian story of salvation through the work of Christ. The second is open to debate. Would a (next) life with all the longing, all the hoping, all the desiring taken out of it be heaven? More like, hell, I think. And the unambiguous first answer, though true, is only true as far as it goes. 'The myth of lost perfection is deep in the Christian psyche' says Christopher Southgate.[10] It is a mistake to say that all longing and the sense of searching for something just out of reach are aberrations from some earlier state of perfection. To be human, to be made in the image of God, is to long for the just-out-of-reach. And our longing is because of how and by whom we are made. Desire is built into the universe. And this mention of desire brings us to something which I hardly touched on in the chapter on the flavours of love. It was indeed the elephant in the room (or, more specifically, the bedroom). Why was there virtually no mention then of sex? And a second question immediately follows: Why introduce sex as soon as the talk has turned to the impossibility of achieving what we long for? Surely it does a better job than that?

Well, one thing at a time. The reason for its absence in the earlier chapter is straightforward. Though most people will feel that it is an indispensable part of a relationship of trust and intimacy, it is better seen as something that both expresses that love and enables it to grow, but which postdates the love itself. I mean this not so much in terms of a sequence of events, as of a sequence of priorities. To be sure, physical attraction may well be the first thing we notice when we are undergoing the world-inverting process of 'falling in love', and in straightforward terms of chronology, it may be the first thing that happens. But the hope is that love will blossom, and if it does, then it seems natural to feel that the love was there, waiting, all along. I began to write this section on the day when there was a partial solar eclipse in the UK – though sadly clouds meant it was not visible where I was. But awe-inspiring pictures were available in real time from the places where the eclipse was total, and not obscured. At that moment, which gives us such a humbling reminder that we are floating on a little ball in the solar system (though we are also a little lower than the angels),[11] the sun was covered by the much nearer moon until it passed by and the full glory of the sun was again released. But while that was happening, the corona of the sun, usually invisible to us, was revealed in all its splendour. If love is that sun, and sex is that moon, then we can perhaps imagine that sex makes visible precious aspects of love which we could not otherwise see. But when the moment has passed, both sun and moon are still there, and the moon, we should note, is illuminated not from within itself, but by love's sun.

But of course we have to acknowledge that this relationship between the two often doesn't work out that way, as John Armstrong says in a splendidly wry passage in the book from which I quoted earlier:

(i)t is evident that sex and love often float apart. This is not surprising when we consider that they are, ultimately, quite distinct parts of life. Sexuality is a comparatively narrow field of passion, intimately linked to physical excitement and orgasm. Lust – especially male lust – is often excited by obvious and rather impersonal attributes. This explains why, according to *Cosmopolitan,* you can make yourself more sexy by putting a little thought into your wardrobe – a recipe which can hardly be predicted to make you more lovable in the long run: the only run that counts, when it comes to love. Qualities which make someone lovable – such as patience, loyalty and cosiness – can even be liabilities when it comes to sexual appeal. And, of course, sexiness, especially in its most blatant versions, often promises nothing at all with respect to love.[12]

There can, I suppose, be degrees to which sex may be divorced from love. But the important point is that according to the proportion to which that is the case, it fails to acknowledge and honour the personhood of the other. And to dishonour the person is to dishonour the creator of the person.

Sex, then, in its right place, is an enabler and, one might say, a fertiliser, of love. But it is not a guarantor of it, and can sometimes stand in its way. Hence its absence in the earlier discussion of the flavours of love. But what now of my suggestion that it comes with the grief of unfulfilment attached? I want to suggest that, paradoxically (again!), the more it is linked to love, relationship and commitment, the more we become aware of its shortcomings. 'If sex is merely a form of pleasant exercise' as John Armstrong disarmingly puts it,[13] then with expectations correspondingly low, it will either fulfil that aim, or if it does not, then not too much of the weight of the universe will hang upon the disappointment. If, however, we invest it with the intention to express the inexpressible, to say the most important things in the world, to go where words fail, and to enable us to become in some way the other person, so united are we, then at the very least we are setting ourselves up for a fall. The higher we aim, the more painfully we may land. In the cold light of the morning it turns out that we are after all two people, not one, and there was more to say than we were able to say. So the grief is this: not that we didn't find ecstasy, but that there is still more of love to be found and expressed and grown into. But why is that a grief and not a joy? The answer to that is, I think, absolutely crucial for understanding what love is. The unexpectedness of love brings immediate joy, but wrapped up in its DNA is the realisation that there is – will be – more, but the 'more' is not now but in the future, even if that future is only a second away. The grief is in the 'not yet', and like a hill-walker finding that there is always another peak to be climbed, we are never quite 'there'. There is always more, and there is no end to the more. I suggested earlier that desire is built into the universe. Now we can add the corollary, that grief at the 'not yet' is also built into the universe. This is not in any way to deny the glory and the God-stamped value of the creation – quite the reverse. But somehow we will have to construct a view of the universe that can find a place for this grief within the truth that, as the first creation account tells us, 'everything that he had made ... was very good' (Gen 1:31). In a moment we will consider what this might imply for the nature and intentions of God as creator. But before that there is one more aspect of this grief that we need to notice.

This is crucial, lest we misunderstand the nature of this grief: grief as awareness of the 'not yet' is forward-looking. It is not the kind of existential sadness that comes from wishing we could return to some half-remembered moment of bliss or ecstasy. Grief and sadness are not the same. The universe runs forward, and if we try to run against its direction we may suffer a nasty fall. Baudelaire's poem *Le Balcon* expresses (in wonderful poetry, to be sure) the impossibility and, I would say, the unhealthiness, of such a backwards-facing desire.

> *Je sais l'art d'évoquer les minutes heureuses!*
> *Ces serments, ces parfums, ces baisers infinis!*[14]
> I have mastered the art of recalling those happy moments
> Those vows, those scents, those infinite kisses.

'Will they be born again?' he asks. The answer seems to be 'no', and the result is a weariness and a sadness that I would distinguish from grief in the specific sense in which I have been using it. Lot's wife looked back, the story tells us, and, having done so, did not fare well (Gen 19:26). Desire, and the grief that comes attached to its 'not yet' is what we have to come to terms with. But when we try to do that we are at least going with the grain of the universe, and therefore in some way with the character of its maker. Christopher Southgate, writing about the theological issues that arise when we consider evolution, and in the case of his book particularly how this affects creatures rather than humans, speaks about the 'values' and 'disvalues' that come as part of the package. You can't have the development of the higher creatures, with their wonderful adaptation to their ecological niches, without a considerable price being paid by other creatures. Some have failed to flourish, countless species have become extinct; many seem to have served only as food for others. Some individuals have even had to function as 'insurance chicks', abandoned once the favoured sibling was seen to be thriving. Of this vastly complex and ambiguous world he writes, quoting terms used by Darwin, '"Grandeur" accompanies the groaning, and the groaning may be the only way by which "exalted objects" may arise'.[15] What is true of evolution – which is the method God appears to have chosen – seems also to be true in the field of existential human experience: as well as all the joy and all the glory, there is as yet unfulfilled longing, and the grief that comes with it. This is absolutely not the result of humans' failure to walk with God as he intends (though we all do fail). No. It was always going to be like this, and joy and grief are built into the universe.

A further thought follows inevitably, though it is a dangerous one. A composer can only write what comes out of his or her own being, and of course the same is true of the work of an artist in any field. Anything else is immediately identified as counterfeit. In the same way, if God is the Great Artist, then we must assume that his creation, in all its complexity and with all its capacity for joy and grief, bears the stamp of his character. We cannot say that God meant it to be different and less problematic. Though humans have certainly messed it up (and we will come in due time to look at the particular mess we have made of the environment), this was always going to be a world and a universe with joy and grief woven in. God's signature is on every atom and in every aching or rapturous or as yet unfulfilled moment.

This chapter has been about 'getting our eye in' – trying to see whether aspects of the world we know may throw up things that might belong in a universe that runs on love. There is no proving to be done here, no triumphant 'I told you so'. We have to go much more cautiously than that, acknowledging, as we saw at the very beginning, that we are only creatures, and that all our knowing must be provisional. But perhaps, when we begin to look, there are ways of seeing the world that at the very least don't run counter to the idea of love being the reason for everything. Now, as I hinted a moment ago, we need to ask a perhaps more difficult question: if the creation has this character and reason and goal, then what can we say of its creator? We need to do that before, in the final section, we can dare to say anything about how all this might affect the way we live, and in particular how we should look after the bit of God's universe that we are responsible for.

4

Love from the Edge of the Universe

L'amor che move il sole e l'altre stelle.
The love that moves the sun and the other stars.
(Dante)[1]

'In the beginning'

Where was *agape* at the Big Bang? Was it just waiting, hiding in the shadows, for the thirteen and three-quarter billion years to elapse between the Great Singularity and the beginning of God's self-revelation to creatures who could respond to him? When we put 'creation' and 'God' into the same sentence, or the same thought, we automatically begin to insert ideas such as power, authority, otherness and so on. 'By the word of the LORD the heavens were made, and all their host by the breath of his mouth' says the writer of Psalm 33 (v 6). 'He spoke, and it came to be; he commanded, and it stood firm' (v 9). Many of the Psalms take a similar view: in celebrating the creation they celebrate the power and authority of God. In particular, the 'word' of God is something that carries a guarantee: if God says so, it will be so. This emphasis on God's power is of course entirely right and legitimate. How could we not think, if we believe in a creator, that his conjuring of things into existence demonstrates his power? But I want to suggest that from a Christian perspective this may not be the whole story.

Incidentally, this reverence for the speaking action of God spilled over in Hebrew thought to the idea that our own words should be treated as sacred, and as having power to bring things about for good or ill. They truly come from Pandora's Box. Hard-pressed and distracted senders of emails sometimes send a second one saying that they 'would like to recall the email with subject x'. This seems a pointless exercise. The deed is done, the thought is out. Press 'send' with care aforethought. Emails are made of words, and as with all words, once they are out, they are out. They cannot be put back in the virtual box. And the cyber-bullies who haunt the world of social media hide behind the apparent anonymity of the virtual world. But their words are no less damaging because of that, as those on the receiving end know to their often enormous cost. Psalm 141:3 asks 'Set a guard over my mouth, O LORD: keep watch over the door of my lips'. And the very next sentence sees the calamitous consequences of unguarded speech: 'Do not turn my heart to any evil, to busy myself with wicked deeds'. Words can be spoken, emailed, and shared on social media – but also written in books, so in this one, as we explore what may be some risky or surprising thoughts, and take up some issues over the behaviour of God, either in acting or (from our perspective) in failing to act, I am aware of the dangers of unguarded words. If I get it wrong, may God have mercy on writer and reader.

So let's return to the question of whether talk of power and so on is the only language we can use in thinking about creation. I think we can say with only slight hesitation that if love only exists when there is action, then it's at least possible that the action of God in creating might be a context within which we might see love. We can't leap immediately to that conclusion, and will need to take some careful steps along the way. But at least we can say that it's not out of the question.

The creation accounts in Genesis don't mention God's love in any way. They focus, as we have also noticed in the Psalms, on the authority of his word. 'God said ... and it was so.' But I think it is legitimate to re-read them and re-evaluate them in the light of Christian understanding. In fact we must do that. Our starting point – and our finishing point – for identifying love is certainly the love that God demonstrates (a verb, as we noted earlier) in the incarnation, life, death and resurrection of Christ. But we must allow our contact with this love to inform and guide all our thoughts about love in every context. The life, death and resurrection of Christ make us redefine everything. Could it be that the new meaning of power is love? Can the new meaning of beauty be love? Can the new meaning of everything be love?

The title of this chapter is, strictly, a misnomer. The concept of 'spacetime' was toyed with before Einstein, but it was his discovery of general relativity that focused it. Though it seems impossible to imagine, space in its three dimensions and time in its one dimension turn out to add up to one concept, which has been called spacetime. Einstein discovered that it can be bent by the influence of mass – the more mass, the more bending. This is sometimes illustrated for our aching brains by the picture of a flat sheet made of some flexible material, and marked with a grid of lines forming squares. When a heavy object like a ball is put on top of this sheet, the lines of the grid near the ball are bent into curves. And the point is that what comes under the influence of this mass is not just space, but time also. As if this were not mind-boggling enough, there is a further consequence: the universe has no edge. Although, as we know, it is expanding, and has been since the Big Bang, it is not expanding 'into' anything – there is no space beyond its edge which it then fills up, and there is no time outside itself that it can catch up with. So, strictly, *agape* can't come to us from the edge of the universe, because there isn't an edge. But perhaps the idea can at least encourage us to 'think big' as we try to comprehend how love might be built into its fabric.

In fact the more accurate picture of a universe that has no edge, and 'beyond' which there is not even nothing, may turn out to serve us well in trying to understand an absolutely crucial aspect of the creation. It brings us directly to the idea of love as an essential or, I think we will discover, as *the* essential component of creation. For shorthand it's referred to by its Greek name of *kenosis*. This is the word that Paul uses in Phil 2:7, where he is quoting a hymn which probably served as an early statement of faith: [Christ Jesus] 'emptied himself, taking the form of a slave'. Here, of course, he is explaining the significance of the incarnation. But during the second half of the twentieth century, some theologians began to develop the idea that this 'self-emptying' could also be seen in God's act of creation. Christianity of course takes the person and work of Jesus as the primary source for our understanding of the nature of God. But as I have pointed out already, whatever we discover of his nature from that source must always have been true. God's character does not change, though the contexts in which he demonstrates it may do. So what is true of God as the one who becomes incarnate must be true of God as the one who creates.[2]

We are now ready – at last! – to look at the flavours of love that we identified earlier in Chapter 2, in order to see if they could have any meaning in the context of God's love as creator. But it's important to have the right background in view, which is where the idea of a universe with no edge may be fruitful. If, as we shall see, there are senses in which God is emptying himself by creating the universe, this is not at all a case of him withdrawing or giving up aspects of himself, or of deciding not to be in the space that he makes for creation and creatures, or of becoming in some way less than he was. Quite the reverse: if there is self-giving, he is giving himself *into* his creation. God is pouring himself into this universe that has no edge. Where he goes, creation goes.[3]

At this point, as we begin to see if we can translate what we know of love from our perspective, into some ideas about what God's love might look like, there is a crucially important proviso to keep in our minds. As we saw earlier, our loves are fitful at best, and constantly marred by our many fallibilities, so we must not fall into the trap of thinking that there is an equality between God's love and ours. We could say that his love is three-dimensional, or, better, multi-dimensional, whilst we live two-dimensional lives at best. But this does not mean that there is no correspondence at all, otherwise we would need to use different words for the two entities, and we would be back with God speaking a language we could not begin to understand. So, acknowledging that caveat, we can be brave enough to ask: what might it be like for God to create in love?

The first thing we will have to say is that if it's love that bears any relation to our loves (and remembering that it is our loves that flow from his, of course, and not the other way round), then it will be costly for God. But what could the cost be for a God who needs nothing and who cannot become less than God by pouring himself out in love? Just this, I suggest: if God could command his creatures to respond with love, then he would be not the loving creator, but some ghastly cosmic psychopath who would demand the correct response and permit no deviation. There can be no love in the universe unless it contains the possibility of the absence of love. It's so easy to invent, for the best of reasons, a picture of a God who gets his way all the time. This seems to do justice to his power and authority and otherness. But we are going to have to learn a new meaning of power. Power turns out to look like giving permission to the other to fail to reciprocate, and yet still to wait, and persuade, and hope, and love against all the odds. The cost of love makes love dangerous for all involved. We live in an age and a society which attempts – probably in part for well-intentioned reasons, though fear of litigation is never far away – to reduce risk and make everything predictably safe. God, in creating out of love, doesn't seem to have been much influenced by Health and Safety. This is something very difficult for us to hear in the early years of the millennium. And, I freely acknowledge, very difficult for me to hear as a parent in a family that has experienced some of the worst that one human can do to another.

So it seems that if God is going to create a universe that can produce creatures capable of conscious response to him, then the possibility must remain open that they may choose not to respond. The cost of love is the terrible permission it must give to the beloved not to love. Coercion, or the insistence that love will be returned, is the suicide of love. If God meant love when he invented the universe, then he was accepting the wager that he might never be loved in return. It's possible, I suppose, that if he had made a universe only of things, and not of sentient and self-aware beings, then perhaps there might have been no potential for rejection. But love seems to demand more, and to need a response. The so-called 'anthropic principle' says that if the starting conditions of the universe had been even fractionally different, it would not have evolved into one capable of producing life. We are here, and able to think these thoughts, and choose whether or not to respond to a creator, only because the universe was set up in a very specific way – for example, in the relative amounts of helium and hydrogen. With even marginally different starting conditions, we wouldn't be here. This is not a proof of course, because one could turn the argument round and say that because we are here, that means that the starting conditions just happened to be such that life was able to evolve, QED. But this is a bleak view of things, which doesn't do justice to the fact that whether we choose to acknowledge it or not, we are living in a world where there seems to be a 'meaning' beyond the cold analysis of facts. I find it more convincing to think that the fact that we are here is intentional – because a creator wanted to express love. And that because of the supreme insistence of love, he was willing to bear the cost.

The side issue of the cost that comes through separation is more difficult to tease out. For an all-knowing God, who is able in some way to be present everywhere and at all times, there is not a direct equivalent to, for instance, the desolation felt by lovers when they are not able to be together. But if we think of God as a parent, then perhaps we can discern some parallel in the pain of allowing the child to become his or her own full self, which involves ceasing, though gradually, to be a dependent child, and grow into an independent adult. The paradox is that, although I am dependent on God for everything, and not least for my being alive, he must allow me to be someone external to himself. Within the mutual love of the Trinity there is no 'other' outside the members of that Unity-in-Trinity. But the act of creating others has altered that dynamic for ever. Now there are beings external to God, and that fact can only be seen as a cost to him. Perhaps that is an infinite cost, but one he is willing to pay for the sake of permitting and enabling a free response of love from his creatures in return.

Finally, in considering the cost to God of setting up a love-universe, there is the huge issue of his forgiveness of us. Any exposition of Christian belief will have as its central theme the wonder of what God has done to demonstrate his love and forgiveness. There will be time later to think in a little more detail about what cost he had to pay, and about one way in particular in which we as a race have failed to live up to what he intended for us. For now we simply note that the permission to us as God's creatures to choose not to respond, or simply to fail to do so through ignorance or inertia, requires at the very moment of creation a commitment to forgiveness. This is not at all to say that he is the prisoner of his character and unable to do other than to forgive. It is to say that the decision to make a universe where love ruled meant that forgiveness would be needed. There is mercy already in creation.

God's love costs him. Perhaps we can ever so hazily feel our way towards the fact that it would have to be like that if love is to be love. More difficult to relate to how it might look from God's perspective is the second flavour of love we looked at, which turned out to be the paradoxical one that it demands exclusivity, but that this is worked out within a social context. Clearly within a human relationship of intimacy and commitment, the beloved holds that position to the exclusion of others. But God doesn't love just you, or just me, so where is the exclusivity? Perhaps we can find a clue in the countless Old Testament references to the fact that God wants his people for himself, and is hurt when they start giving some or all of their allegiance to 'other gods'. (We brushed past this idea in Chapter 2.) Jealousy has come to mean for us in modern parlance something akin to mistrust and suspicion of infidelity, or to the wish to have something that someone else has and I haven't. But in Hebrew usage it is more to do with God knowing that his people will get on best if they respond to his love and don't start toying with the practices associated with heathen gods. In other words, it contains a heavy dose of love, if that is seen as wanting the best for them.

So he wants each of his creatures to respond to him (though as we saw a moment ago, he is not allowed by the rules of the game to force the issue, lest love be killed by coercion). He wants me, not in distinction to you, but in distinction to any other 'god' I might think would cut me a better deal. And then, just as human exclusive relationships operate and only flourish within a social context, so his wish is for all of humankind to be united because of their relationship to him. But you might well object that this is just too idealistic to be of any value – clearly what I have outlined isn't how it's going, and the direction of travel isn't going to change any time soon. As we saw in Interruption II 'Too Much to Ask?' the gap between such an idealised picture of how things were meant to be and how they actually are is so great that we can be forgiven for thinking that the mess is the only reality and that love was never part of the picture.

Surely God could do a better job, and in particular could have created a world that didn't have the potential to go so horribly wrong? J. Austin Baker has written an important book called *The Foolishness of God*. At the end of a closely argued passage on how the world might be if it had been set up so that there were no pain, whether that be physical or existential, he says this:

> If someone's death causes me no pang, is it possible for me to care about them? If no word or act of mine, or of anyone else's, no accident of nature, no defect in themselves, can cause pain either to them or to me, can I have any concern for them? In short, to our list of losses do we have to add – love?[4]

The kind of love we are beginning to discover is the only kind there can be. With all its potential and permission for disaster, and with all its insistence on exclusivity, there is no other way. It appears that if the universe is, by God's decision, to be ruled by love, then once he has made that decision he has to renounce whatever methods he could in theory have used to make sure the whole thing went well.[5] It is the only way for him to be God. And that brings us immediately to the next flavour of love.

The next thing we identified, and for which we now need to find a God's-eye version, is that to love is to hold oneself back, but this leads to the enlargement of self. So we must ask if this holding back from forcing the issue is the only way for God to be God, and if there is any meaning to the idea of God enlarging himself. On first sight, it feels as if applying this idea to God would be to make him no God at all. Isn't God supposed to be complete, perfect, 'unimprovable'? Well, if we unpick the idea of perfection, we might be in for a surprise. Christianity, and Western thought in general, is (still) so hugely influenced by Plato that we often miss his looming presence. His big idea was that if you went far enough behind any thing or any concept, a bit like a philosophical version of Windows, you would come to the 'perfect' version of it – though this was never one that could exist in the 'real' world. It follows that these perfect versions of everything could not change. So perfection was a static concept. But this isn't what it feels like to be alive. In the story of our own lives, we don't think of trying to arrive at some place of perfection. Much rather we think of trying to grow, or develop, or become. These are all verbs of action, and I suggest that that is what life is like. We're never going to 'arrive' at some end-point, after which there would be nothing to do other than contemplate our perfect navels. And if as Christians we think we're on the way to 'heaven' (though, as we shall recall later, there's precious little about that in the Bible, but rather a lot about a new heaven and a new earth) then who wants that to be an endless sitting about with no further progress possible? If we're all going to be playing the harp (which I doubt) then it would be horrifically dull if we knew we couldn't get better at it because we were perfect performers already.

If life for us is a process, and a never-to-be-finished journey, then I think there is reason to believe that it's like that precisely because we are made in God's image. It's what he is like – or, more accurately, it's what it is like for him to be who he is. But how can I possibly have the effrontery to suggest that I know what it's like for God to be God? Well, clearly, as I was careful to point out in the Preface, we must hedge every thought concerning God about with humble agnosticism and an acknowledgement of our mere creatureliness. But, if we dare to say anything at all, and here we come back to love, if he made us in his love so that we could respond in love, then it seems reasonable to think that the creatures he made for this destiny would bear some relation to his own being. Otherwise the response could not have any meaning. Gods we are not, for sure, but we are made in the image of God, and are, as I noted earlier, (only) 'a little lower than God' if we choose to translate Ps 8:5 in that way. So I think it is fair to suggest that just as existence for us feels like a process and not a state, it may be like that for God too. (Although really, as I said, the logic is the other way round – existence for us is as it is because of how it is for God. Again: we are made in his image – a staggering thought – not he in ours.) Referring to the suffering that comes as part of the package where love is concerned, Paul S. Fiddes writes the following two jaw-dropping sentences: 'We can say that in the transforming power of love God uses even suffering to fulfill God's own being, becoming more truly who and what God is. In suffering through desire to bring many sons and daughters to glory, God completes the divine glory as well.'[6] Except that I would want to suggest that that process will never end for God, as it never will for us. Mutual love gives birth to a process of becoming, and who would want that ever to stop?

If the meaning of the universe is love, then, as St Paul says in his hymn to love in I Cor 13:8, 'love never ends'. And the growth, not towards static perfection but simply 'towards', will never end. 'Farther up and farther in' as C. S. Lewis beautifully puts it at the end of *The Last Battle*, the final book in the Narnia series.[7] We are caught up in the direction of the universe. And if we will allow it, there will always be more to see, more to discover, more to become. But the path to enlargement of self lies through suffering – for us and for our maker.

This might all sound as if, however rocky it may be, the path is already laid out, and all we have to do is keep walking. But the next flavour of love that we identified is that it is experimental. This, as we saw earlier, is closely linked to the costliness of love. There seem to be no guarantees. We may wager everything and lose everything. But if we don't accept the wager then the one sure thing is that we won't win anything.

Does God then do wagers? And if the answer is yes, then dare I trust him? Well – I think the answer to the first question is indeed 'yes' and to the second is 'I have no alternative – *if* I am risking everything for love'. J. Austin Baker puts it like this:

Unless we have faced the radical question which … the fact of suffering puts to us, and have *already* [his italics] made the naked choice to hold love, sacrifice, concern, and the rest, of greater value than exemption from pain, we cannot rationally believe in a God of goodness at all ... This is the necessary logical order of events: commitment to love first, faith in God second.[8]

We could develop this idea by saying that the universe only makes sense if we decide that love is what governs it. This book is, I hope, suggesting some reasons as to why that 'naked choice' is rational and supported by evidence. But ultimately we just have to decide that we will walk through this life, in this world, in these circumstances, whatever they may be, on the basis that love is what fires it and gives it its significance.

This, then, is the wager: I may be wrong, but as there is only one go at it, I will decide in favour of love. I will decide that God can indeed be trusted.[9] I will wager that that is the best, and perhaps the most rational, decision even if it is the case, as it looks as if it is, that God has risked no less than everything for the sake of creating a universe of love that can contain creatures able to respond to him. So what risks has he taken – and is still taking, since the universe is still, and always, being made into what it has the potential to be? Well, is it not the risk that everything might go wrong, and, having gone wrong, might not be susceptible to being mended by love? We are so used to relying on the love of God that we easily come to view it in a different way from how we view love in other contexts. In all human contexts, we can only love and hope. We cannot love and guarantee. As we have seen already, something that calls itself love but accepts no possibility of failure or rejection is not love at all. So why should it be any different for God?

But to ask this dangerous question appears to suggest that his power is not infinite, and his will is not irresistible. But that is where the logic leads us. I suggest that God has decided, if one may say this respectfully, to make the 'naked choice' for love. He could have done otherwise, but the supremacy of his invention of love means that he has decided to forgo his prior rights, and risk everything, even failure, for love. Paul S. Fiddes puts it like this: 'In making a free world that can lapse from divine purpose, God is exposed to the risk of something that God does not directly create.'[10]

This is terrifying. Am I proposing an emasculated God, who can only 'do his best'? In spite of what we know of his intentions through the incarnation and crucifixion of Jesus, are even these only the last throw of the dice, with the outcome still uncertain? Is love really so powerless? Well, as I suggested at the beginning of this chapter, perhaps we have to learn a new understanding of power. The kind of power that can be married to love is not coercive, but trusts love to do the job. And at that point we have to stop, because we cannot know for sure that love will do the job. But it's the only hope we have. We, and God, must make the naked choice.

We cannot leave this look at the experimental nature of love without considering how the resurrection may alter the equation. We will look later (Chapter 5) at how the resurrection of Jesus points us to the resurrection, not just of ourselves, but of the whole of redeemed creation, with huge implications for how we live in it and look after it. But to give the briefest possible response for now, we could perhaps say that God, having risked everything and died in the attempt, is vindicated by the resurrection as the one who as it were claimed in advance that love was worth it and would outlast the worst that could happen. Had there been no resurrection, there would have been no meaning to being a follower – into the future – of the prophet who died in just the same way as many another troubler of the Roman status quo. The resurrection is the only reason we have for viewing the death of Jesus as different from any other undeserved death. But even if we can arrive at this point, it seems that there are still no guarantees. We still have to weigh up the evidence for the resurrection, and then make the wager that that fact alters everything. There is plenty to hang onto as we decide in favour of love, but the whole thing is still an experiment.

Finally, we must investigate how the last characteristic of love that we identified might work out from God's perspective: what is the significance for him of the fact that love is about relationship and must have an object? This is perhaps a difficult question to answer, not because the concept is so far from what we think we know about God, but for the opposite reason that it may seem so obvious that there is not much we can say beyond a platitude. Of course God wants a relationship with his creatures. Isn't that the whole point of the Christian story? Isn't the whole thing usually presented in terms of God having acted to heal and restore a broken relationship between his creatures and himself? These things are true, of course, but let's see what happens if we go back a step or two. In fact we need to go back as far as we can, rather in the way that cosmologists try to understand the earliest moments of the universe. We are trying to make out, however dimly, something about the 'why' of creation. What thought on the part of a creator could possibly have led to the existence of everything that there is? – and not just the 'stuff', but the ideas, the desires, all those things that seem to lie just beyond our reach, but which we know instinctively must be there and which somehow tell us that we are not accidents and that there is meaning to the word 'meaning'. I said earlier, in discussing the relationship flavour of love, that 'love cannot exist without an object, and it cannot exist outside the orbit of a relationship'. If this is true, then there are huge implications for what it meant for God to create, and with this I think we have come to the sharpest point of our search so far. For love to come into existence, it had to have an object. *No universe, no love.* Or at least no evidence for love, and no object for it. Without those, it really can't be said to exist. It is not that the universe has made possible a lot of love, but that love has made possible a

76

lot of universe – everything that exists, 'seen and unseen' as the Nicene Creed puts it. And not just possible, but necessary. If, as Paul says in Col 1:16, 'all things have been created through him and for him', then this was so that there could be love, so that he could have a creation to love and which could return that love. This invests the creation with infinite value. And there follow from that, as we shall see, huge implications for how we live in the creation and how we look after it.

But can this really be the case? I am suggesting that God was obliged to create, not because of some compulsion outside himself, but as the direct result of his decision to invent love. To create was the only way for him to bring love into existence.[11] The 'naked choice' for love demands that there be a creation. The fact that we are here at all, wrestling with this stuff, points ultimately to the love that rules the universe. Keith Ward puts it like this:

> If one thinks that 'God is love' (1 Jn 4:16), that love is an essential property of the divine nature, and that love can only be properly exercised in relation to others who are free to reciprocate love or not, then the creation of some universe containing free finite agents seems to be an implication of the divine nature.[12]

Of course, the creation is much – very much – more than us humans. We must not be unduly anthropocentric. Bishop James Jones is right to remind us of '(t)he connectedness of the human family with and within the whole of the created order in heaven and on earth'.[13] Each part of the creation celebrates its creator in its own way, and according to its own nature, as we shall shortly see. And yet, and yet, a universe without creatures able to respond to God by conscious decision would be a poor container for the love of God. It would not permit the two-way nature of love without which love is not fully love. But if there are human creatures who can respond to him, then the rest of the creation assumes vast importance, for we know that without the rest of it we would not be here. Evolution tells us this, of course. And we know that the vast size of the ever-expanding universe points to its immense and unfathomable age, and that that age is required for evolution to have done (and still be doing) its work. Whatever position we may happen to take on the possible existence of life, and perhaps intelligent life, elsewhere in the universe, it is certainly the case that for humans to have evolved has required the whole of the universe. Nothing that God made is redundant.

But to return to the two-way aspect of love, we can see that it has another implication. God apparently wants to be known, and even wants his creatures to be the ones who can 'satisfy (his) needs and desires', as we saw in Chapter 2 when thinking about human love. But does God really have needs? Dare we think this? Well, no less a theologian than Vincent Brümmer thinks so: '(W)e long for the love of others because as persons we necessarily *need* to be loved. But can we say the same of God?... If, as we have argued, God *desires* our love, it would seem to follow that he also *needs* our love for this desire to be fulfilled.'[14] I mentioned earlier, (note 5), that we need to be careful not to suggest that love 'precedes' God, or that he is in some way beholden to it as a force outside himself. In the same way, we need now to assert that God's 'needs' do not precede him, as if he suddenly realised that there was some external force acting upon him, and therefore acted under their influence. Just as it seems more exciting to think of God inventing love, so here it seems a fruitful idea, and a thrilling one perhaps, to suggest that God has chosen to have needs, and that those needs should be of the sort that could only be satisfied by the responsive love of creatures.

If there is to be love, there must be a universe. And if God chooses to make himself known as love, he must allow his creatures to satisfy his need for responsive love.

Interruption III: Too Much Theory?

In the chapters so far, I have tried to show that there is evidence, in spite of all signs to the contrary, and although there will never be proof, that if the universe were founded on love, it would have to look like the one we live in. Our human loves can help us understand something of what God's love must be like, if it is to be anything that we are able to recognise as love. And we have seen that for love to exist there must be a universe, and it must contain creatures who can recognise and return the love of God.

If we have reached some temporary staging-post in this journey of discovery, then I must acknowledge that the means of getting here has been mostly in the head, though I hope there has been a measure of heart-involvement as well. We have had to step back a little, and take a long look at our human loves, which have then shone some light on what it may mean for God to love. As well as requiring a certain amount of abstraction, it will also not have escaped the reader's notice that there has also been relatively little so far about the one who, Christians believe, supremely shows the love of God in action – the one who, as John says, is the eternal Word who 'became flesh and lived among us' (Jn 1:14), and whom the writer to the Hebrews describes as 'the exact imprint of God's very being' (Heb 1:3).

More of that soon, in Chapter 5, but for a moment we can allow ourselves a little time to admire the view – a view of the love which we are beginning to see, in spite of the all-too-present mess that we see around us, as the reason for the creation, and of the love whose ever-expanding growth is the goal of that creation. This can perhaps act as a counterbalance to the necessarily thought-out process that has allowed us to get this far. After that, we will see in a final section if we can bring what we have found about a love-universe, as well as our thoughts on the incarnation, life, death and resurrection of Jesus, and our own experience of the world as it is, into some kind of harmony that might give us a reason for taking radical action to care for the world. But first let us avoid abstraction, look around and get a little practice at seeing love where we might have missed it.

> *Krone des Lebens, Glück ohne Ruh,*
> *Liebe bist du!*
> (Goethe: *Rastlose Liebe* – Restless Love)

> Love, you are the crown of life, joy with no rest!
> Arise, my love, my fair one,
>> and come away;
> for now the winter is past,
>> the rain is over and gone.
> The flowers appear on the earth;
>> the time of singing has come,
> and the voice of the turtle-dove
>> is heard in our land.
> The fig tree puts forth its figs,
>> and the vines are in blossom;
>> they give forth fragrance.
> Arise, my love, my fair one,
>> and come away.
> (Song of Solomon 2:10-13)

It is no accident that this glowing biblical love poem intermingles human love and the flourishing of the creation. We are made of the same stuff that everything is made of, and God's purpose is for each part of the creation to fulfil its destiny, according to its God-given nature. Commenting on the early chapters of Genesis, Pope Francis, in his Encyclical *Laudato Si*, wrote 'These ancient stories, full of symbolism, bear witness to a conviction which we today share, that everything is interconnected, and that genuine care for our own lives and our relationships with nature is inseparable from fraternity, justice and faithfulness to others'.[1] When we love, we begin, however falteringly, to be in step with the universe, and when we are in step with the universe our loves are able to live.

I have the privilege, one that is denied to many, of having a garden behind our suburban London house. Some years ago, the church that my wife and I are members of put on an 'open gardens' weekend, to raise money for a good cause. A friend was given the job of writing a short paragraph about each garden, for the enlightenment of visitors. In the case of our garden, he explained with splendidly dry humour that behind a shed, and mostly out of sight until you went down a short connecting path, was a hidden 'minimal intervention' garden. We were rather proud of that, since our intention was to have turned what had been a neglected and purposeless area into something that felt natural, and approximating to what one might hope to find in the countryside. But to achieve something that looks 'natural' in fact requires some work – the 'tilling' that Gen 2:15 describes as God's purpose in putting humans in the garden of Eden – otherwise it would quickly turn again to the dull and unloved patch that we saw when we first came to the house. I am sure that we have been only partially successful, but although it is certainly a work in progress, it is a place that seems calm in spite of its urban setting, and is home to some interesting wildlife. Here is a tiny fragment of the universe – the universe which is invested with infinite value. Can I see love here, or is that just some romantic and ultimately contentless idea that would disappear as soon as any pressure was applied to it, like putting a pin to a balloon?

I suggest not. A few months ago I was watching leafcutter bees take up residence in a small hotel (as I like to think of it) made from narrow open-ended bamboo pipes, which sits between two branches of an old apple tree. They could be seen cutting tiny circles from the edges of some raspberry leaves, just bigger than the size of the pipe. Having put in a fertilised egg, and leaving it with a loving gift of nectar and pollen, they painstakingly sealed up the entrance by gluing the piece of leaf in place. A few weeks earlier, the same hotel had been occupied by mason bees, which, instead of a piece of leaf, blocked up the entrance with mud. In this way they could protect as many as six eggs, each with its own compartment. And I learned that the eggs that would turn into females went in first at the back of the pipe, and those that would be males were nearer the end, ready to hatch out first. Wonderful are the ways of nature. But did you choke over my use of the phrase 'loving gift'? Surely the bee was merely doing what bees do, amazing though it is. How could anything it does be 'loving'?

Well clearly it couldn't, in any conscious way. But, for all that it is unconscious of self, and acting according to instinct, perhaps we can see some parallel with the way a human mother cares for a growing child both before and after birth. It does not at all demean her role to say that when acting in this way she is acting according to instinct, or that the child grows within her with no conscious effort on her part, other than paying the best possible attention to her own health, upon which the health of the unborn child depends. So I suggest that our bee, though unable to express love consciously, in some way acts in love by acting according to its nature. There are hierarchies of love, and the highest of them is love freely expressed and received between human and human, and between human and God. But the world in which this is possible is also a world in which other creatures, acting according to their natures, can express their part in a universe that has love in its DNA.

To put it another way: It would be wrong to suggest that I was watching love in some quasi-human form, but it would be equally wrong, or perhaps more so, to say that what I was watching was an absence of love. It is there if we choose to see it. The universe hums to that frequency. This was just one example, of course, and there is an infinite supply of others, if we can develop a taste for it. We are learning to speak the language.

I wish I'd listened more in science lessons at school. Back then, as an aspiring pianist, I was of the opinion that music was the most important thing I could focus on, with languages and the arts in general following a little way behind, and other subjects not much more than also-rans. It's true that to develop one's skills as a professional musician requires a lot of time and effort, and there probably isn't time, and most of us don't have the skill, as I said earlier, to be good at everything. But looking back from the considerable distance I now am from my school days, I think I was half right, but not more: music is fantastically important to human flourishing – but so, I would suggest, is everything else. It's possible to see music as a glorious thing that contributes to a world set up by love; it's also possible to learn about the wonders of the universe and see them as examples of the action of a loving creator. If we choose to do so, we can imagine love wherever we look, however confused and paradoxical the situation may be, and in all the countless things that human creativity and curiosity and imagination can find. Perhaps this is what Paul had in mind when he suggested 'whatever is true, whatever is honourable, whatever is just, whatever is pure, whatever is pleasing, whatever is commendable, if there is any excellence and if there is anything worthy of praise, think about these things' (Phil 4:8). This is absolutely not an invitation to turn a blind eye to trouble or disaster or the agony that attends our lives, but to view those things as happening, for whatever reason, in a world that was set up so that there could be love.

Gerard Manley Hopkins was able to see through things to their essence, and celebrated not just the created order, but, as in his poem *Pied Beauty*, the worth of what humans are able to do within this invented world. He gives glory to God for the beauties of the created world, and for 'Landscape plotted and pieced – fold, fallow, and plough; / And all trades, their gear and tackle and trim'.[2] The created order can praise in its own way, and in so doing returns love to its maker. Plough and tackle point us to the dignity of work, and in this case the dignity of caring for the earth. This too can be love received and given if we choose to let it be.

It will be as well to keep all this in mind as we now turn to think about the possible connections between the life of Christ and an earth that is the theatre of our loves and God's. If this earth is where we love and are loved, and where God has made himself known as love, and where Jesus went about doing good, then we cannot understand his mission of love unless we understand his relationship to the earth.

5

Down to Earth

Great little one! whose all-embracing birth
Lifts Earth to Heaven,
stoops Heaven to Earth.
(Richard Crashaw)[1]

'How silently'

Christianity's early flirtation with Plato and Greek philosophy
was disastrous, and continues to be so. We saw (in Chapter 4)
that his ideas of perfection encouraged early Christian thinkers
to imagine heaven, and the God who lived there, as static and
unchanging. His character is unchanging, to be sure, in the sense
of him being reliable and trustworthy. But if he is shut off from
our experience of change and momentum and development,
then we are not going to be able to have much of a relationship
with him. A further idea follows logically if we give any air-time
to Plato's imagined static perfection: it is known as dualism,
and suggests that the 'spiritual' is of greater value than the
'physical' – or even, in its more extreme manifestations, that the
physical is inherently evil. These ideas were explicitly rejected
by the Council of Nicea in 325 with its famous proclamation
that the Father is 'maker of heaven and earth, of all that is, seen
and unseen'. But the virus lived on, and lives still, in ideas of a
soul somehow hampered by a physical body and waiting to be
released, of a disembodied heaven that we're heading for once
we have got rid of the annoying body, and even, in its most
extreme form particularly in right-wing American circles, of a
welcoming of environmental disaster as the precursor of the
return of Christ – except that this is understood in non-material
terms and involves the end of all things physical.

I suggest that Christianity is much more earth-affirming than this. There are plenty of reasons, not the least of which is the physicality of the resurrection. Bishop James Jones says 'to the Jewish mind with its holistic attitude to creation, in stark contrast to the dualism of Hellenistic philosophical systems, there was no resurrection conceivable that did not include the body'.[2] We will think further about the resurrection in a moment, but to begin with we need to see what connections can be made between Jesus and the earth.

The first connection is so obvious that we could miss it: God has apparently invested a huge amount of time and effort (if one may use such language) in bringing into being the universe that includes the earth to which Jesus came. The first chapter of Genesis says that his verdict was that it was very good. We have no mandate to suppose that he revised his opinion. The many Psalms that celebrate the glories of creation tell the same story. Psalm 104 is a joyful description of teeming life and, as we might now think of it, an ecosystem that makes possible the ongoing and ever-developing story of life. 'You cause the grass to grow for the cattle, and plants for people to use, to bring forth food from the earth, and wine to gladden the human heart, oil to make the face shine, and bread to strengthen the human heart ... O LORD, how manifold are your works! In wisdom you have made them all; the earth is full of your creatures' (vv 14-15,24). But there is more. Who was (and, we should be aware, is) doing the creating? Looking back after the resurrection, and trying to make cosmic sense of his experience of three years in the company of a prophet, but much more than a prophet, John describes him as the *logos*, the Word, through whom 'all things came into being' (Jn 1:3). To any educated Jew or Greek, this idea of *logos* was no revelation: everyone who knew anything about Plato knew that the *logos* was the principle behind what we understand by goodness, and the reason for the rationality of the world – the fact that we can discuss it at all. The bombshell is not these opening verses of John's Gospel. He is setting us up to be assaulted by the devastating assertion that 'The Word became flesh and lived among us' (v 14). This is shocking and world-inverting, however much all the pretty Christmas cards and warm carols may try to convince us that it's cuddly and comforting. The one through whom the earth was created came here! This is Christianity's Big Idea. Apparently this oh-so-physical and material world is one that can house its creator. If this idea seems normal and not to be surprised at, then either we never understood it in the first place, or, having understood it a little, we have learned not to be overwhelmed by it.

It's easy to see how this can happen. Musicians, by the demanding nature of their craft, are obliged to practise for hours in order to master a new piece and find ways of filtering the composer's imagination through their own. I sometimes like to tell students that in some ways it's a pity that we have to do this – though there is clearly no alternative. Familiarity may breed, if not contempt, then at least a forgetfulness to be amazed. There is a lovely little Sonata for Violin and Piano in E minor by Mozart (K304), the only one of these that he wrote in a minor key. The second of the two movements is a graceful and unassuming little Minuet. After a while it trickles to a halt and there is a silence. Out of that silence there appears, and in the key of E major, a tender and heartfelt melody played first by the piano, then echoed by the violin, which is more like a hymn than something out of a secular, domestic piece. I can still remember, though it is more years ago than I care to count, the amazement and the joy that accompanied my first experience of that moment, when I was playing the piece through, having never heard it before. And if I play it now, I try to retain that 'first fine careless rapture' as Robert Browning so hauntingly expressed it. A musician's job is precisely this: to convey to the listener a freshness and wonder as if he or she were hearing it for the first time. But this is difficult to do, precisely because in order to get it just right, it must be practised and rehearsed over and over again, with all the danger of over-familiarity that this risks.

It can be the same with the Incarnation. How can we recapture the sense of wonder at this invasion of 'our' world by the one to whom it belongs? We certainly need to try to do that if we want to connect the life of Jesus to the love that created the world. We will come soon enough to his death, which Christians believe supremely demonstrates the lengths to which his love was willing to go. But to have that in its right place, we must first see him walking on the earth that came into being, along with 'all things', through him. Jesus' feet got dusty with the dust he had made.

The only title that Jesus used of himself was 'Son of Man'. Bishop James Jones has explored this imaginatively in his book *Jesus and the Earth*, from which I quoted a moment ago. He points out that although Jesus may have had in mind references from the Psalms, Ezekiel and Daniel, it is possible that he could also have been referring to the early chapters of Genesis. 'In Hebrew the phrase 'Son of Man' is Ben Adam, Son of Adam, and Adam is the one hewn from the earth, A*damah* in Hebrew.'[3] James Jones goes on to look at numerous verses where 'earth' is mentioned alongside 'Son of Man'. Whatever we may make of these, it's unequivocal that Jesus lived as a member of what we might now call a community of smallholding farmers, who worked to grow enough food for their immediate needs, and it's likely that he was also a carpenter, with skills rooted in the fertility of the earth. He knew a connection to the earth, with its rhythms and its profound simplicities, that we in the so-called developed world have all but lost. And, we might note, the footprint on this earth of the one through whom it had been created was a zero-carbon footprint.

It was from his connection to the rhythms of a simple and earth-respectful way of life that Jesus took almost all of his parables and many of his other sayings. He spoke about planting seeds, tending sheep, growing vines, catching fish, pruning plants, making bread, and much more. But there is an important point to note here. It's easy for us in our partial disconnection from the earth to assume that these parables just happen to use such illustrations because they were near to hand, and were about practices and events familiar to his hearers. That is certainly true as far as it goes, but there is a more profound thing going on. They are indeed illustrations, but they are more than illustrations too. They show us the truth because, if only we can have ears to hear and eyes to see, these things in and of themselves embody that truth. If everything that exists comes in some way from the hand of a God who is love, then there can be nothing that does not in its own way reflect and embody that love. So for instance what is true of yeast is true of how God's kingdom grows (see Lk 13:20-21). Each in its own way bears the one stamp of the one who made everything. The connection of Jesus to the earth was not just a handy way for him to have a supply of parables that he could use to explain the kingdom, but was in itself part of the coming of that kingdom. He started his ministry by saying 'the kingdom of God has come near' (Mk 1:15). The kingdom is not disembodied, separate from the earth on which it was proclaimed. The kingdom was near because the one whose kingdom it is was walking on the earth, and taking all of creation into himself and into his incarnated life. If you want to talk about kingdom, then everything is kingdom. Seeds are kingdom, and allegiance to the Word made flesh is kingdom. If you want to talk about love, then everything is love. Plants are love, and the self-giving of Jesus even as far as death is love. You just need the eyes to see it.

However we need to be careful: I would not want to spoil the point by overstating it. These embodiments of love and of God's intentions as creator and then as redeemer are not equivalent in weight and import. Clearly the self-giving on the cross of the Word made flesh is love at greater weight – and, truth to tell, at a weight greater than we know how to bear or respond to – than the love that is built into the life of a plant. But, although they are at very different points in a hierarchy of love, they are, if one may put it like this, from the same stable.[4] It hardly needs pointing out that the death of Jesus was all too physical. Real wood, real nails, real agony, real death. This was a death that happened in this created world. Edward P. Echlin says: 'The life, suffering, death, burial and resurrection of Jesus, Lord of climate and evolution, was and remains at the very centre of the earth.'[5] Here for all to see is the cost of love.

Countless others wiser than I have meditated, thought, written and spoken about the salvation that we believe was achieved by Jesus on the cross, and I do not feel adequate to add to that body of understanding and inspiration. But the point to make here is that this all happened on the real earth, in real time, to a real human being. This was the cost of Jesus' total and irrevocable connection to the earth. If this was the cost of love, then in some way it was a cost that we creatures can relate to. Clearly not in one sense, because we cannot know what it was like for the Word to be separated from the Father and the Spirit. (Here words become inadequate and perhaps less than no words at all.) But we know what pain is, and most of us know what rejection feels like. We should not be surprised that the greatest art is about tragedy. The connection of Jesus to his love-creation led inevitably to the cross, and, as we have seen already, love only exists when there is action.[6] 'God's love was revealed among us in this way: God sent his only Son into the world so that we might live through him. In this is love, not that we loved God but that he loved us and sent his Son to be the atoning sacrifice for our sins' (I Jn 4:9-10). God did not shout from a distance, but came into the world. As I said, if this seems in any way unsurprising, then we have missed the point.

But, Christians believe, that is not the end of the story. This broken and defeated Jesus was laid to rest by some of his devoted followers, his body as convincingly dead as that of any other human who has died. Humans on earth die, whether that be through natural or unnatural causes. The followers of this one, however, found an empty tomb, and met a resurrected master. I cannot put it better than Tom Wright. Giving a rationale for the rise of the church and the potency of its claims, he writes:

> Far and away the best historical explanation is that Jesus of Nazareth, having been thoroughly dead and buried, really was raised to life on the third day with a renewed body (not a mere 'resuscitated corpse', as people sometimes dismissively say), a new *kind* of physical body which left an empty tomb behind it because it had 'used up' the material of Jesus' original body, and which possessed new properties which nobody had expected or imagined but which generated significant mutations in the thinking of those who encountered it. If something like this happened, it would perfectly explain why Christianity began and why it took the shape it did.[7]

There's plenty of literature, and rightly so, on the historicity of the resurrection and on what follows if it is true. The issue for our purposes, as we think about the connection of Jesus to this very physical world, and about how this might allow us to see love in action, is the strange nature of the resurrection appearances. Apparently he was difficult to recognise, and yet when he was recognised, it was obvious. John records that the first appearance was to Mary Magdalene, who mistook him for the gardener. This was entirely rational, though someone trying to invent a story in first-century Palestine wouldn't have had a woman as the first witness, or even the second or third. The world was the same, and yet also utterly changed. Mary recognised him when she heard the love in his voice as he spoke her name (Jn 20:11-18). People who had known him well, such as the two disciples on the road to Emmaus, could be with him and yet not realise who it was, until the light rushed in (Lk 24:13-35). Then they couldn't believe that they hadn't recognised him straight away. But we shouldn't be surprised by all this, I think. Dead people don't come back to life (or at least, in Jewish thought, not until the end of all things when all the faithful would rise together and God's reign of peace would begin). The problem to get your head round was the idea that one person, but not everyone, had risen, and yet the triumphant reign of peace didn't look as if it had begun. This hadn't been forecast, so it would not have been anywhere near their list of explanatory options. And then he could come and go at will. With no warning, he could disappear from the sight of the two, and then again with no warning be amongst the other disciples, the larger group meeting in fear behind locked doors back at Jerusalem, and calm their terror with the simplest of words, 'Peace be with you' (Lk 24:36). A Jewish follower of Jesus, well-versed in expectations of what would happen at the end of time, really couldn't make this up. Jesus could give fishing advice to outdoor, down-to-earth men who had spent their lives learning their trade, and then cook them breakfast and eat with them (Jn 21:1-14). You can smell the smoke.

All this is the breaking-in of the new order ahead of its completion. Though we have only a tantalising glimpse, the new order is going to look something like this. Jesus was recognisable but in some way freed from the constraints of physicality. If, as Paul says, Christ is 'the first fruits of those who have died' (I Cor 15:20), then 'all will be made alive in Christ' (v 22). What we have fleetingly seen as true for him after his resurrection will be true for us. It will be God's affirmation of his love-commitment to his creation. It is nothing less than the remaking of this so-earthy first order, and in which, just as was the case with the resurrection of Jesus, the first creation will be the raw material of the new creation, resurrected and remade. Christianity is unashamedly physical.

Some years ago I played the organ at the funeral of a saintly old lady who had been a stalwart of a church which I had attended many years before. The preacher delivered a sermon which made a deep impression on me, but sadly for all the wrong reasons. His chosen passage was Revelation 21:1-4, the famous passage about the new heaven and new earth, where God will wipe away every tear. There was precious little about the wiping away of tears, which might have offered some comfort to the grieving family. What there was a lot of was the assertion that the passage means that believers are going to heaven. I toyed with the idea of letting out a low blast on the organ, but fortunately decorum and a strict upbringing from long ago got the better of me. To quote New Testament scholar Tom Wright again: 'There is almost nothing about 'going to heaven when you die' in the whole New Testament. Being 'citizens of heaven' (Philippians 3:20) doesn't mean you're supposed to end up there.'[8] The passage from Revelation says (in poetic language, to be sure) that John saw 'the holy city, the new Jerusalem, coming down out of heaven from God' and that 'the home of God is among mortals'. The preacher seemed happy to tell the congregation that this meant that when we die we will go up to heaven (if we were believers). I suggest that this is not what it says. Believe it or not, it seems that John is saying the opposite. He imagines the New Jerusalem coming down out of heaven to the earth, and the home of God being among mortals. This is where the universe is going, and it's going there because its meaning is love. The Old Testament contains many shadowy hints about a coming age of peace, when God will reign over a transformed earth. The catalyst for this seems to be a son who will be a king and inaugurate this new age. If these half-articulated longings found fulfilment in the coming of Jesus, then we are truly between the ages. Meanwhile, as Paul says, 'the creation waits with eager longing' (Rom 8:19).

James Jones puts it like this:

Many Christians still sit loose to this understanding of the gospel, preferring to see the priority in saving souls for heaven. But the biblical hope for the future involves a new heaven *and* a new earth. Just as there is a continuum between the bodies we now inhabit and our spiritual bodies in the future, so there will be a continuity between this earth and the new earth. The Kingdom that Jesus inaugurates is the one where heaven finally comes down to earth. It is the earthing of heaven in a new heaven and a transformed earth that consummates the central petition of the Kingdom Prayer – the coming of the Kingdom through the doing on earth of God's will as it is done in heaven.[9]

This is where the universe is going, and it's going there because its meaning is love. There is more to come, and there will always be more to come. For this reason, as we saw earlier, and using the word in the rather specialised way I suggested then, there is grief – but not sadness – built into the story. Grief at the 'not yet'. Will there ever be a time when there is no longer any 'not yet'? Perhaps in the end grief will be swallowed up by joy, but that must be a joy that permits more joy to be still to come. Here, I think, we reach the end of what we can conceive, and must fall silent before the intentions of a God of love.

At this point, and perhaps lowering our sights just a little, it's important also to observe that the promise is not just for humans. As well as being much more physical than we may have been told, Christianity is also far less anthropocentric than we have been led to believe. Eph 1:10 says that the plan is 'for the fullness of time, to gather up all things in him', and Col 1:20 is similarly explicit in asserting that 'through him God was pleased to reconcile to himself all things'. The Greek *ta panta* is unequivocal and allows no exceptions. It cannot have its arm twisted to mean 'all people' (though even that would raise some interesting questions about whether ultimately it is possible for anyone to remain outside the embrace of God's love). It can only mean everything that has ever existed and will ever exist. All this will be gathered up into the love of God. This is no small religion. Its scope is beyond our comprehension, just as the universe itself is bigger than we can conceive of, and contains mostly stuff that we apparently have no way of observing. And this cosmic reach of what God intends to achieve out of his overflowing love was not some idea that appeared in the New Testament with no preparation. Hos. 2:18 contains the astonishing promise that 'I will make for you a covenant on that day with the wild animals, the birds of the air, and the creeping things of the ground'. This picks up another much earlier covenant promise, made to Noah after his adventures in the ark. Suggesting a new significance for the rainbow, God tells him that 'This is the sign of the covenant that I make between me and you and every living creature that is with you, for all future generations' (Gen 9:12). If the scope of what God intends to do doesn't take our breath away, then again we have probably missed the point.

These connections of Jesus to the earth, and the cosmic dimensions of God's purposes to which they point, will, I hope, enable us to enlarge our imaginations. But if they remain there, they will sooner or later fade into the dullness of routine, or the distance of forgetfulness. To keep our imaginations alive, we must allow them to change the way we live. This is the work of the Spirit of God, since we cannot do it on our own. So in that spirit, or Spirit, we are ready now to consider one area in particular in which the way we live might be directed by an awareness of the love that began the universe, and continues to hold it together, and will bring it to completion.

6

One Minute to Midnight

To see a World in a Grain of Sand
And Heaven in a Wild Flower,
Hold Infinity in the palm of your hand
And Eternity in an hour.
(William Blake)[1]

'The maker's masterpiece'

This book has been about learning to see love. We can only experience love, and return it to others and to the creation and to God, in and by virtue of the physical world we live in. 'No universe, no love'. This world is what God has invented as the place in which love could be seen, and touched, and cultivated. His invention of love requires a physical universe for love's existence and growth, and he has invested everything in it, and risked everything for it. The creation is the cauldron of his love. This is reason enough to care for it. But this is not a dully utilitarian argument: we are to care for the creation simply because God made it and loves it, not just because it is the place that sustains us and where we do our loving. This should be obvious, but we humans misuse the gift either because we do not identify it as a gift, or because we think that, once given, it is ours to do what we like with. But it is not ours to possess. By what logic can I go from saying 'without the earth I could not exist' to 'the earth that allows me to exist is mine'? The one absolutely does not flow from the other. And Christians would of course have to say that in terms of ownership, its maker must be the only one with a title to it.

However, Christians have been shamefully, and possibly disastrously, slow to connect their faith to the needs of caring for the planet. This, I am sure, is mainly due to the emphasis, to the exclusion of a wider picture, on personal salvation as a ticket for entry to a disembodied eternal future in heaven. As I have tried to show, this is not an adequate picture of what God has achieved in Christ, or of what he intends to achieve. Christ died for me, and you, but he also died to reconcile all things to God. And in his resurrection we can see the first glimmerings of what the new heaven and the new earth will look like. Our job now is to live out the intentions of God. In the high but challenging words of St Teresa of Ávila (1515–1582):

> Christ has no body now on earth but yours. No hands, no feet on earth but yours. Yours are the eyes through which he looks with compassion on this world. Yours are the feet with which he walks to do good. Yours are the hands through which he blesses all the world. Yours are the hands, yours are the feet, yours are the eyes, you are his body. Christ has no body now on earth but yours.

Paul imagined the creation as 'groaning in labour pains' (Rom 8:22). This was a hopeful vision, pointing towards its redemption which was now in view thanks to the coming and awaited return of Jesus. But he could have had no inkling of the depth of this earth's groaning as we and it still wait in the twenty-first century. The average temperature of the earth's surface has increased by at least 0.85° C in the last 100 years, and probably by 1°. According to NASA, sixteen of the seventeen warmest years since such records began 136 years ago have all occurred since 2001. The concentration of CO_2 in the atmosphere is now higher than at any time in the last 800,000 years and has set a record high each year since records began in 1958. Now it is true that natural events like El Niño have the effect of drawing more CO_2 into the atmosphere, but it remains the overwhelming scientific consensus that human activity is the prime cause of these increases, which are happening probably 100 or 200 times faster than when the earth emerged from the last Ice Age. I am writing this as the Caribbean is being assaulted by one of the strongest hurricanes ever recorded, with loss of life and almost unimaginable damage to property and infrastructure. Those whose job it is to forecast and comment on such events are rightly unwilling to say that any specific example of extreme weather is directly caused by global warming, but it is beyond dispute that global warming will make such things more common, and their effects more intense and deadly.

Since 1900, sea levels have risen by an average of about 19 cm. The rate of sea level rise has accelerated in recent decades, placing a number of islands and low-lying countries at risk. The polar ice sheets are retreating. There is evidence that with less ice, less heat is reflected back away from the earth. This is what is known as positive feedback, where one effect causes another, which in turn redoubles the presence of the first. Scientists have determined that if temperature rises go beyond 2° C compared to pre-industrial levels, this will lead to substantial and dangerous climate impacts, which will hit the world's poor in particular. We have already contributed one of those two degrees, or very nearly.

Not only that. Evolution happens with unimaginable slowness. In the long history of the earth, species have come and gone, and each has found an ecological niche to which it was adapted. But that adaptation takes countless generations to come about. Many of those adaptations have been on account of changes to the climate, with all the associated changes of habitat and weather. There have indeed been many changes in global temperature and climate conditions in the long, slow history of life on earth, and species have slowly adapted and changed. The problem with human-induced global warming is that it is happening too fast for species to adapt. World Wildlife Fund scientists have estimated that most species on this planet (including plants) will have to 'move' faster than 1,000 metres per year if they are to keep within the climate zone which they need for survival. Many species will not be able to redistribute themselves fast enough to keep up with the coming changes and so may well become extinct.[2] This would be a tragedy for certainly sufficient aesthetic reasons: a loss of biodiversity is a loss to us who are able to delight in the fecundity of the natural world, and, one would have to add, a loss to its maker. But there are more practical reasons for trying to prevent this. Some of the species that might struggle or fail to survive are intimately bound up with food production, such as pollinating insects and predating creatures that feed on other creatures that feed on our crops. So there is a strong argument from self-interest, or self-preservation.[3]

The COP21 Conference on global warming in Paris in December 2015 was predicated on trying to limit temperature rise to no more than 2°C in global temperatures. Towards the end of the second week, there was a concerted and successful move to lower this aim to 1.5°, which felt like unexpected and welcome progress. The decision of President Trump to withdraw the US from this agreement in 2017 felt like a body-blow to those who had celebrated after the Paris Conference, and to the earth itself which is our only home, though it has perhaps galvanised many to act with more speed and determination. But even a rise of 1.5° would risk dangerous and unpredictable effects, with the only safe prediction being that the poor would come off worst. They are at greater risk for two reasons, which combine lethally. They, and their countries, are less able to meet the costs of dealing with the effects of global temperature rise; and they tend to live in areas that will be more seriously affected, particularly in terms of sea level rise and extreme weather systems that start over the oceans. Many of the world's poor live at sea level. In years to come, patterns of food production will change, water will become even more scarce in some areas than it is already, and extreme weather events such as floods, storms, heat waves and droughts will lead to loss of life and large-scale forced migration.

Issues of climate change, therefore, are entangled with issues of justice. At the Paris conference, one of the main sticking points was the understandable wish of developing countries to get rich by the same method that allowed the developed West to get rich – by burning coal. Where was the justice, their thinking went, in the rich countries telling us that we can't do what they did? Where was the justice in them saying 'do as we say, but not as we did – and are still doing'?

This all seems worse than gloomy. And it is true that the situation is desperate, and time is running out. If action is not taken soon, then we may be completely unable to deal with the consequences. In terms of still having the opportunity to fend off at least the worst consequences of climate change, we are at one minute to midnight, and the clock is inexorably ticking. Creation is groaning louder than ever before, and we have made it so. But Christianity is nothing if not full of paradoxes. So in this dark context we also hang on to the hope that God will not abandon his project, but somehow bring it to completion in the new heavens and new earth. This hope must be rooted first in God's *chesed*, his loving faithfulness, and then in the universe-changing consequences of the cross and resurrection. If Christianity paints a true picture of things, then the first, revolutionary, shout that 'Jesus is Lord' is still true.

Do we then sit on our hands and wait? I think not. How would that be a response of love – to creator, fellow human and fellow creature? Love only exists when it is doing something. Christian hope is not just a private attitude for the individual, but something that encompasses all creation. And for those who claim to have been touched by the love of God, it is a call to action. Because we live in the paradoxical age of 'now' and 'not yet', we are to live out the values of the coming new heaven and new earth now, and in so doing we inaugurate what will be fulfilled in the future. And, I would suggest, we hasten its arrival.

If, following St Teresa, we are to be the hands of Christ, then only the most overwhelming of motivations can hope to give us the courage to take the action we need. We have that motivation in the contemplation of a universe designed for love by the God who is love, and destined for completion at the time of its remaking. But that knowledge or awareness brings with it the most terrifying responsibility. In the mysterious but uplifting passage that we noted a moment ago, Paul seems to link the future of the creation to the 'revealing of the children of God' (Rom 8:19), for which he says the creation is waiting 'with eager longing'. The context seems to imply that the children of God are those who are 'joint heirs with Christ'. If we are the ones who have 'tasted that the Lord is good' (1 Pt 2:3), then a primary way we respond must be in how we care for the creation of the God who made it for love.

In the first few centuries CE, Christianity was seen as a threat to what we would now call the establishment, and this was largely the case until the 'conversion' of the Emperor Constantine in 313, when it became the official religion of the Roman Empire. Until then, that first statement of faith that 'Jesus is Lord' was a direct threat to the cult of worship of the Emperor. How the times have changed! And not necessarily for the better. We are certainly not called to seek confrontation, and we are called to honour the role of government as the means whereby justice and freedom are able to flourish. But God also calls us to 'have no other gods before me' (Ex 20:3). I suggest that one of the alternative gods that we must speak out against, and against which we are to live in contradistinction, is the great god of economic growth. I am aware that this is a cornerstone of capitalist economics and of other models of economics too. But if we can just step away for a moment, it doesn't seem too difficult to see that 'growth' requires increasing use of the earth's resources. Those resources, however, are finite. So much should be obvious. It is therefore not too much of an intellectual leap to realise that growth in this sense cannot continue for ever. We will run out of resources. Maybe not tomorrow or the next day, but constantly increasing growth cannot continue for ever in what is a closed system, that is to say one which has specific limits of capacity. We can do nothing unless the earth permits it.

If this sounds like the naïve ideas of someone who should stick to his own area of expertise, then I call as witness Pope Francis. In his Encyclical *Laudato Si* (subtitled, we should note, 'On care for our common home') he wrote:

> if in some cases sustainable development were to involve new forms of growth, then in other cases, given the insatiable and irresponsible growth produced over many decades, we need also to think of containing growth by setting some reasonable limits and even retracing our steps before it is too late. We know how unsustainable is the behaviour of those who constantly consume and destroy, while others are not yet able to live in a way worthy of their human dignity. That is why the time has come to accept decreased growth in some parts of the world, in order to provide resources for other places to experience healthy growth. Benedict XVI has said that 'technologically advanced societies must be prepared to encourage more sober lifestyles, while reducing their energy consumption and improving its efficiency'.[4]

The conundrum is how to lift the poor out of grinding poverty whilst conserving the earth's resources. Whatever else that may involve, it will certainly not happen without a curtailing of the developed world's greed.

The Global Footprint Network[5] estimated recently that the earth is now consuming the equivalent of 1.6 planets, and if things continue as they are, that will be 2 planets' worth by the

2030s. August 2 2017 was 'overshoot day' – the day by which, since January 1, we had used a year's supply of the earth's resources, viewed in terms of how quickly they can renew themselves. This day comes earlier each year: in 2000 it had been early October. The date compares humanity's demands, such as carbon emissions, land for crops, stocks of fish, and the use of forests for timber, with the planet's ability to regenerate these resources and absorb the carbon emitted. And of course the so-called developed world is using by far the majority of these resources, and is responsible for the larger part of the overshoot. The Network's website publishes an overshoot day by country – showing what would happen if all the countries of the world used the earth's resources at the same rate as the featured country. It makes sober reading, particularly as the circle of dates takes us pretty accurately from the most 'developed' countries, (the earliest dates) to the least 'developed' (the latest dates). This puts the situation into stark focus.

After Peter's sermon on the Day of Pentecost, many of those who heard him asked 'What should we do?' His uncompromising reply was 'Repent' (Acts 2:37-38). So if privilege brings responsibility, we must do the same, and repent of our careless use of the earth's finite resources. Christians should be at the front of the environmental movement, but we certainly have not been. It's true that enlightened individuals and groups have been ploughing a lonely and courageous furrow,[6] but the church in general has, at least until recently, kept its mouth shut and its hands in its pockets. The church of which I am a member has been investigating the possibility of installing solar panels on its large roof. At a meeting of the PCC (Parochial Church Council) I said that the recent decision of the UK government to reduce hugely the 'feed-in tariff' (the amount paid per kilowatt-hour generated) meant that we would not be able to do this in any expectation of getting our money back – but that I still believed it was the right thing to do. Sadly, we had received advice from our Diocese that it was 'not keen on solar panels unless they were hidden'. I suggested that this was mistaken for environmental and theological reasons. We have to do better than this otherwise we cannot claim to have been touched by the love of a creating and redeeming God.

The primary responsibility for demonstrating how to care for creation lies with those who believe in the God of the Old and New Testaments. Our Jewish heritage tells us as early as the first chapter of Genesis that we are to care for the earth that sustains us, and that message continues through the Psalms, the wisdom literature, the prophets, and the historical material that sets out how the people were to treat the Promised Land. Our Christian heritage tells us that God's redemption through Jesus is for the whole universe. We are the ones who believe we have tasted the love of God at first hand, and claim to know by what motivation and for what purpose the world was made. And, we must add, we are the ones who believe that God's good purposes will ultimately be fulfilled. So this call to action and responsibility comes with hope attached. This is the meaning of the resurrection.

But this is not exclusivism. Quite the reverse: Christians must join with all who care about this precious earth, and there are many. We have seen the love of God in the face of Christ. Others, responding, if one may respectfully put it like this, to a lesser light, have nevertheless seen clearly what we should have seen all along, and it is to our shame that they saw it first. The desire to care for the earth is hidden deep in the human heart, and there are many who have allowed this deep wisdom to take root in their lives and lead them to action. The worldwide marches ahead of the Paris COP21 conference were an inspiring moment – tens of thousands of people across the world expressing their desire for a better-organised world. Many came from a variety of faith backgrounds, and many doubtless had no commitment to religious belief, but just a deep human awareness that the earth is precious and that we owe it to those who come after us to pass it on in a healthy state. If we are all children of a loving creator, then we are truly all in this together, and Christians had better be humble enough to acknowledge the huge contributions of others to the present levels of environmental awareness. But two years later this sense of urgency and the belief in the possibility of action is under strain, though as we have noted, the US's withdrawal from the Agreement may yet galvanise again those who had such hopes in 2015.

And Christians had better not think that we have exclusive rights to being the people God is willing to use to achieve his loving purposes. The Old Testament is full of stories in which God used people who had none of the direct connection to him that his chosen people claimed to have. Moses' life was saved by the daughter of a pharaoh (Ex 2:1-10); Cyrus, King of Persia, who facilitated the rebuilding of the Temple, was called The Lord's anointed (Is 45:1); Ruth was a Moabite, but features in one of the genealogies of Jesus (Matt 1:5). The Jewish people were slow to learn that God can use whoever he chooses to fulfil his plans, and as Christians we have been similarly reluctant to widen our view of how God might choose to do things. If we chip away the centuries of imaginative accretions to the story of the Magi who visited the young Jesus, we know little of them except that they were outsiders and followed the light. But the point remains: if as Christians we believe in a God of love, then we have a motivation not available to others. We had better act on it. In the words of Pope Francis: 'Living our vocation to be protectors of God's handiwork is essential to a life of virtue; it is not an optional or a secondary aspect of our Christian experience.'[7]

The question of exactly how we should act on this motivation is a complex one. But this complexity is not beyond the skill of God to untangle, and to pass on to those who seek his wisdom. In Proverbs chapter 8, Wisdom is personified as a female figure

(Sophia in Greek). 'Ages ago, I was set up, at the first, before the beginning of the earth' (v 23). She is pictured as 'rejoicing in (God's) inhabited world and delighting in the human race' (v 31). Here wisdom is explicitly linked to the wonder of the world, and implicitly to its care, including the care of those who live on it. If Christians believe that the Spirit is available to all, and is the one through whom God makes known his will, then we had better listen to his, or her, wisdom.

It's very easy to think that the issues are so huge, and so global in their import, that only politicians with the power to make laws and formulate national and international policies can do anything significant. The Paris COP21 Conference was a triumph of negotiating skill, and perhaps its most important legacy will be that for the first time nearly two hundred countries acknowledged the need to act together to prevent disastrous global warming. The intention (though not the promise) to reduce temperature rise to 1.5º was an unexpected result, taking commitments beyond what had been prepared in the weeks and months before the conference began. Another positive result may be that investors will begin to see renewable sources of energy as a safer place for their money than polluting and carbon-emitting ones. In the September 2017 government auction of energy sources in the UK, new offshore wind generation required a subsidy not much more than half that required by new nuclear.[8] The issue in the years to come will be whether individual governments are able and willing to do what they have said they mean to do – the US's withdrawal is specific and hugely dispiriting, but all the other governments still need to take tough action and make hard decisions. Will vision become limited, and will global concern be overtaken by local self-interest? We must pray not. There is limited time to put things right, as the Paris conference acknowledged. But governments need a helping hand from their citizens, so they must be called to account. In the years after Paris, the pressure must be kept up. We owe that to the poor and disadvantaged, to those who will be most affected by climate change, to those who worked so hard to bring at least some harmony amongst the many countries taking part in the conference, and above all to the earth's creator.

Now it is one thing to call for people-pressure from the relative safety and freedom of the UK, quite another to ask it of those who live in less open societies. But whatever it will look like, if there is to be any hope of preventing the worst consequences of our former greed and unwisdom, then action must, as it were, come from the bottom up as well as from the top down. Those in positions of power and influence will only act if they feel they are responding to, and then have the support of, an overwhelming groundswell of public opinion. It is our responsibility to change the culture.

It will require the collective wisdom and inspiration of many to work out the practicalities. Whether, for instance, my decision not to fly on holiday to a relatively poor country does good by reducing carbon emissions (though doubtless the plane will still have flown there) or does harm by not bringing trade to its inhabitants. And if, to mitigate my guilt, I arrange for some trees to be planted, or donate money to an environmental project, would it still have been better not to have flown? I have solar panels on the roof of my house, and so generate a certain amount of electricity that is sent to the grid for use by all. But clearly this is a tiny and almost unmeasurable fraction of the requirements of the UK population, let alone of the world. And then there is the issue of agriculture. Cows contribute 3% of Britain's greenhouse gas emissions and at least 25% of its methane, which is 23 times more potent as a greenhouse gas than CO_2. In New Zealand, where cattle and sheep farming are major industries, 34% of greenhouse gases come from livestock.[9] If significant numbers of people became vegetarian, or at least ate significantly less meat, these effects would be reduced. But what would become of the livelihoods of the farmers? And of course the landscapes that we are inclined to think of as natural, and the biodiversity that some of them support, are in many cases the direct result over many centuries of grazing by livestock. Are these the prices that the world must pay? In material terms, the individual can do very little. But the power of many acting together can change the culture, and it is this that must happen if specific physical changes are ever going to be made. Somehow the world must learn to live more lightly. In the words of Micah, we must learn 'to do justice, and to love kindness, and to walk humbly with our God' (Mic 6:8).The church is called to work with all those who can see that to do this is the only way to save the planet.

There are of course countless other ways, and an infinity of moments, through which we can take forward God's intentions of love. But it seems to me that if we fail in caring for the earth that he made to be the place where love can supremely be expressed, then we may have difficulty in bringing love to other areas of our lives as well. Caring for God's creation is not a hobby in relation to more weighty matters of belief. Our relationship to the earth must be at the heart of our relationship with the earth's maker. And as far as earth's inhabitants are concerned, if we fail to care for the place where they live, and where they receive and return their loving, then we are failing to care for them, and especially for those more at risk. God has given us the privilege of being his co-workers in filling his universe with love. If we have begun to see his love and to return it to him, then we will begin, however falteringly, to love what he loves, and act accordingly.

7

Creation and Cross

for love in creation,
for heaven restored,
for grace of salvation,
O praise ye the Lord!
(Henry Williams Baker)[1]

And all shall be well and
All manner of thing shall be well
When the tongues of flame are in-folded
Into the crowned knot of fire
And the fire and the rose are one.
(T. S. Eliot)[2]

'Now and not yet'

The job is begun, but not finished. We live our lives in tension between the glory of creation and the agony of the cross. This is how it is for us, because this is how it is for God. The love that willed the universe into being is the love that took Jesus to the cross. This is the forgiveness that, as we saw earlier, is built into the very concept of a love-inspired universe – but remembering again to be clear that this love that has forgiveness as its inevitable companion is a love willed into being by God, and not imposed upon him. Only then can we speak, as we must, of love and forgiveness and grace in the same breath. It is inescapable that from the moment of creation this would be the destiny of God. Love was always going to pay the ultimate cost (see Chapter 5, note 6). For reasons that are beyond us now to fathom, and will perhaps remain so hereafter, there was no other route to the resurrection, and therefore there was no other route to the renewal of all things and the final triumph of love. The coming into being of the new heaven and new earth depends utterly on the coming, living, dying and rising of Jesus. This was the cost that God undertook to pay by the very act of creating. There is a wonderful moment near the beginning of Bach's great *St Matthew Passion*. The soprano soloist sings words that translate as 'he loved them to the end'. A single phrase moves from high to low, looking back up momentarily but then renewing its downward flow. In just twelve simple notes Bach was somehow able to express the heartbreaking mercy of God in coming to his creation, but also the infinite cost of that commitment, which was built into the fabric of the universe when God invented love and made a world that could be love's home.

But if there is a tension between creation and cross, then that tension is overseen by hope. The hope is that what became true for Christ in his resurrection will in the end be true for each of us and for all creation. Without the resurrection, we would only be able to make a blind guess in answering the question as to whether God's launching out in love would in the end be fruitful and fulfilled; or fruitless and in vain, with all the cost, and the permission for love to turn away, reaping a harvest of disappointment. But because of the resurrection, we have reason to hope that love, though never coercive, will win the day. And it is for all creation: nothing God does or makes goes to waste. That is not to say that everything goes in a linear, orderly progression to its final fulfilment. We know enough of the tragedy and pain of the world to know that the picture is much more confused that that. But the resurrection tells us that in the end, love will have the final word.

Philip Larkin's evocative poem *An Arundel Tomb*[3] reflects on the fourteenth-century tomb of a couple who had been an earl and a countess. In the final stanza he writes:

Time has transfigured them into

Untruth. The stone fidelity
They hardly meant has come to be
Their final blazon, and to prove
Our almost-instinct almost true:
What will survive of us is love.

The last line is often quoted out of context as an expression of some kind of certainty, but Larkin is suggesting something quite different: that though we might wish it to be otherwise, it is likely that our hope for love to survive will ultimately be disappointed. Even he longs for it to be true, but cannot quite bring himself to believe it. It is only 'almost true'. In contrast, I hope that this brief exploration of love as the founding principle of the universe has provided some justification, in both our minds and our hearts, for thinking that love absolutely will survive. It will survive because God has risked everything for that to be so. It will survive because God has allowed love to cost God his very life. It will survive because the creation, made for love, will be remade. Love will survive because God is love.

The tension between the creation and the cross is built into what it must be for God to be God, if love is to have the final word. But it is also built into the fabric of the universe, so that our lives too are caught between glory and grief, between confidence and despair, between longing and fear. And, truth to tell, it often doesn't feel as if love is the source and the goal of our joys and sorrows. But if that is what it is, then it seems that this is what the universe must look like. If we want certainty and a risk-free life, then we will be disappointed. We would need a different universe, one that would play by different rules. But if we are willing to do as God has done and risk everything for love, then he may be able to surprise us. And the intertwined longings of God and of ourselves to love and be loved, will be brought together in the man who was God and also one of us. This is love in the raw, but at the same moment love more refined than we can conceive.

I hope that on this journey of exploring love we have made a little progress in learning the language. In learning to see love where we might have overlooked it. In finding a reason for hope, which is not whistling in the dark, but being drawn blinking towards the light. In linking love to the earth, as God has done. The universe is tingling with the love that brought it, and is still bringing it, into being. But the deepest longing of our hearts tells us that this is just the beginning. If we could see now the intensity of love that will give life to the new heavens and the new earth, we would be utterly consumed by it. We must wait before we are able to venture close to the sun.

But while we wait, we receive and return love. At times we may do that in the warm light of certainty. More often we will do it as children learning to walk, and falling more than we stand. But love will still be there. If there is not love, then there is nothing. But if there is love, then God got it right, and we shall live.

Footnotes and References

Preliminaries

1. I have used the pronoun 'he' to refer to God. As we are beginning to realise, there are problems with this, and not only for those whose experience of men in general and fathers in particular has been difficult or worse. (The same could apply to the use of a female pronoun too, of course.) And the transference to God of the very human idea of gender at all merely exposes our difficulties in speaking meaningfully about God. However, attempts to solve the issue such as using the word 'Godself' seem to draw attention to the problem rather than the person. It is often more helpful to think of God as a parent, but unfortunately we have no non-gendered pronoun to use in that context. So I would ask for the reader's patience if we use the time-honoured, but now perhaps time-limited, 'he'.

2. The idea of persuasion in the context of love was first suggested to me by Keith Ward and Paul S. Fiddes in their respective chapters on 'Cosmos and Kenosis' and 'Creation out of Love' in *The Work of Love, Creation as Kenosis*, ed. John Polkinghorne, published jointly in the United States of America by Wm. B. Eerdmans Publishing Co, and in Great Britain by Society for Promoting Christian Knowledge, 2001. The phrase itself is used by Keith Ward on p. 162. I am grateful for the publishers' permission to reproduce it.

Chapter 1

1. Lewis Carroll, *Alice's Adventures through the Looking-glass*
2. W. H. Auden, *As I walked Out One Evening: Songs, ballads, lullabies, limericks and other light verse*, selected by Edward Mendelson, Faber and Faber, 1995, p. 63
3. C. S. Lewis, *The Four Loves*, Geoffrey Bles, first publ. London, 1960

4. We should remember, of course, that the original conversation probably took place in Aramaic. But in being so specific about the Greek he uses, John is surely giving us the true flavour of it.

5. C. S. Lewis, *The Four Loves*, Geoffrey Bles, first publ. London, 1960, pp. 16-17

6. The highly erotic 'Song of Solomon' is not in the Old Testament canon by accident, and neither is it there primarily as a slightly embarrassing allegory for Christians to use for the love of God seen in Jesus. It can probably be put to that use, but only because in its first meaning it is about the glories of human love.

7. Arthur Peacocke, The Cost of New Life, in *The Work of Love, Creation as Kenosis*, ed. John Polkinghorne, published jointly in the United States of America by Wm. B. Eerdmans Publishing Co, and in Great Britain by Society for Promoting Christian Knowledge, 2001, p. 41

8. Trevor Dennis, *Sarah Laughed: Women's Voices in the Old Testament*, Society for Promoting Christian Knowledge, 1994, p. 56

Interruption I

1. I have written about this at greater length, under the pseudonym Peter Longson, in *God in the Dark*, Wild Goose Publications, 2012, p. 105 ff

Chapter 2

1. Alexander Pope, *An Essay on Criticism*, Part II 1711

2. Another implication of Pope's quotable quote is that it doesn't matter too much how we behave, since God will handily live up to his billing as the forgiver. This finds an echo in the alleged death-bed words of the German Romantic poet Heinrich Heine: 'Gott wird mir verzeihen, das ist sein Beruf.' God will forgive me – that is his job. Such

cynicism will not serve us well on this search for love; but the point about the possible chasm between humans and God remains.

3. By 'creatures', of course, I mean primarily humans. But we shall see later that it may be possible to speak of love in the context of other creatures and even the (to us) inanimate creation.

4. Peter Longson, *God in the Dark*, Wild Goose Publications, 2012

5. Vincent Brümmer, *The Model of Love*, Cambridge University Press, 1993, p. 8 He is quoting Sallie McFague, *Metaphorical Theology*, Fortress Press, 1982, p. 15

6. Vincent Brümmer, *The Model of Love*, Cambridge University Press, 1993, p. 172

7. *Penguin's Poems for Life*, selected with a preface by Laura Barber, paperback 2007, p. 77. Extract from *Walking Away* from Selected Poems by C. Day Lewis reprinted by permission of Peters Fraser & Dunlop (www.petersfraserdunlop.com) on behalf of the Estate of C. Day Lewis.

8. John Armstrong, *Conditions of Love: the Philosophy of Intimacy*, first publ. Allen Lane, The Penguin Press, a publishing division of Penguin Books Ltd, 2002, first American edition 2003, p. 36

9. Peter Longson, *God in the Dark*, Wild Goose Publications, 2012

10. John Armstrong, *Conditions of Love: the Philosophy of Intimacy*, first publ. Allen Lane, The Penguin Press, a publishing division of Penguin Books Ltd, 2002, first American edition 2003, p. 144

11. *'I say I'll seek her'. The Oxford Authors: Thomas Hardy*, Oxford University Press, 1984, p. 97

12. The English language, usually so rich, is poor in this context. We have only the verb 'to know', whereas French has connaître and savoir, German has kennen and wissen,

and Italian *conoscere* and *sapere*. I am of course using the English in the sense of the first of each of these – to know a person, as opposed to a fact.

13. For a defence of this position, see Christopher Southgate, *The Groaning of Creation*, Westminster John Knox Press, 2008, Chapter 2.6, and Peter Longson, *God in the Dark*, Wild Goose Publications, 2012, Chapter 2, the section entitled 'God of the Blank Cheque'. The idea of a lost paradise lies deep in much Christian theology, partly due to Christianity's early and unwise accommodation with Plato. From there it has leaked into Western culture, finding perhaps its most well-known expression in Haydn's oratorio *The Creation*. The music is gloriously inventive and often light-hearted, but the words are a different matter. They use the words of the Genesis 1 creation account and the Psalms, but also draw on Milton's *Paradise Lost*. It was all doubtless well meant. But I see no reason to give free ammunition to atheist-scientific critics of Christianity in the early twenty-first century by proclaiming (as just one example, and as if we still believed it) 'Straight opening her fertile womb, / the earth obeyed the word, / and teemed creatures numberless, / in perfect forms, and fully grown. / Cheerful, roaring, stands the tawny lion. / With sudden leap the flexible tiger appears'. I rest my case.

Interruption II

1. *Fair House of Joy*. A song by Roger Quilter.
2. This region was also affected by a severe earthquake in October 2015. More than 300 were killed, of whom at least 200 were in Pakistan.
3. As suggested perhaps by the title, at least, of the iconic UK television series from 1973 'The Ascent of Man' by Jacob Bronowski.

Chapter 3

1. *God's Grandeur. Poems and Prose of Gerard Manley Hopkins,* ed. W. H. Gardner, Penguin Books Ltd, first publ. 1953, p. 27

2. Peter Longson, *God in the Dark,* Wild Goose Publications, 2012, p. 152

3. Karen Armstrong, *The Case for God,* The Bodley Head, 2009, p. 6

4. Luke Bell, *The Meaning of Blue,* Second Spring, an imprint of Angelico Press, 2014, pp. 21, 39

5. We will come, much later, to a discussion of what it might mean to speak of God as Creator and as Love in the same breath. For now, let us accept it as a premise that might allow us to explore the connection, if there is one, between God's creativity and ours – or, rather, between ours and his.

6. In fact, the 'normal' matter that we are familiar with is quite rare in the universe – estimated at 5%, in stark contrast to the 68% of so-called dark energy, and 27% of dark matter.

7. This is the theory of how matter and energy behave at the atomic and sub-atomic scale – in other words, the theory of the very very small.

8. First broadcast in the UK on 18 December 2011, on BBC2.

9. Set as a song with piano by Roger Quilter. *The Complete Poems of Percy Bysshe Shelley,* with Notes by Mary Shelley. Modern Library Edition 1994. All rights reserved under International and Pan-American Copyright Conventions. Published in the United States by Random House, Inc., New York, and simultaneously in Canada by Random House of Canada Limited, Toronto.

10. Christopher Southgate, *The Groaning of Creation,* Westminster John Knox Press, 2008, p. 36

11. Ps 8:5. Or even, as the NRSV has it, a little lower than God.

12. John Armstrong, *Conditions of Love: the Philosophy of Intimacy,* first publ. Allen Lane, The Penguin Press, a publishing division of Penguin Books Ltd, 2002, first American edition

2003, p. 136

13. John Armstrong, *Conditions of Love: the Philosophy of Intimacy*, first publ. Allen Lane, The Penguin Press, a publishing division of Penguin Books Ltd, 2002, first American edition 2003, p. 137

14. Set as a song with piano by Debussy: no 1 of *Cinq Poèmes de Baudelaire* (1889).

15. Christopher Southgate, *The Groaning of Creation*, Westminster John Knox Press, 2008, p. 2. Later, p. 109, he says: '(T)here is grandeur as well as tragedy in this view of life. The nonhuman world possesses its beauty *because of* [his italics] the processes that also involve the sufferings associated with predation and parasitism and which engender extinction.'

Chapter 4

1. Dante, *The Divine Comedy*: Paradiso Canto xxxiii 145

2. For the following thoughts I have been greatly helped by the various contributors to *The Work of Love, Creation as Kenosis*, ed. John Polkinghorne, published jointly in the United States of America by Wm. B. Eerdmans Publishing Co, and in Great Britain by Society for Promoting Christian Knowledge, 2001.

3. For clarity, and importantly: this is not pantheism, which says that in some sense the universe *is* God; but pan*en*theism, which says that God is everywhere *in* the universe, and that it could not exist, or continue to exist, without his continuing intention. The Son 'sustains all things by his powerful word' (Heb 1:3).

4. J. Austin Baker, *The Foolishness of God*, first published in Great Britain by Darton, Longman and Todd Ltd, 1970. First issued in Fontana Books 1975. Reprinted in Fount paperbacks, 1979, p. 66

5. I deliberately said that it is God's decision that the universe be ruled by love. Here I take issue with 'process theology',

which in this context would seem to say that God had to obey a pre-existing state of affairs, which was the pre-eminence of love. I find it considerably more thrilling to think that love is love because God chose it to be so. He is not the victim or puppet of his own character. As we saw a moment ago, the fact that he forgives is because of his own self-imposed decision to make love the guiding principle of the universe. Love didn't invent God. God invented love.

6. Paul S. Fiddes, 'Creation out of Love', in *The Work of Love, Creation as Kenosis*, ed. John Polkinghorne, published jointly in the United States of America by Wm. B. Eerdmans Publishing Co, and in Great Britain by Society for Promoting Christian Knowledge, 2001, p. 173

7. C. S. Lewis, *The Last Battle*, first publ. The Bodley Head, 1956. Published in Puffin Books, 1964, p. 156

8. J. Austin Baker, *The Foolishness of God*, first published in Great Britain by Darton, Longman and Todd Ltd, 1970. First issued in Fontana Books 1975. Reprinted in Fount paperbacks 1979, pp. 72-73

9. This is, of course, an extension of Pascal's famous wager, set out in section 233 of his *Pensées*, published after his death in 1662. He proposed the idea in the context of a decision as to the existence of God, viewed in the light of the benefits to the individual if he does exist. It is perhaps less self-interested to think of making the wager in the context of deciding whether to live by the conviction that love is at the heart of everything. In God's case the wager is to risk everything – even the success or failure of the project – for the sake of having a universe that runs on love.

10. Paul S. Fiddes, 'Creation out of Love', in *The Work of Love, Creation as Kenosis*, ed. John Polkinghorne, published jointly in the United States of America by Wm B. Eerdmans Publishing Co, and in Great Britain by Society for Promoting Christian Knowledge, 2001, p. 188

11. I have not forgotten the mutual love which, we are told, has always existed between the persons of the Trinity. It is sometimes suggested that this mutual love between Father, Son and Spirit means that God did not create out of any need, for all-sufficient and all-satisfying love was already present in himself. I do not find this entirely convincing. We believe in one God, not three, and make a separation at our peril. The title of Júrgen Moltmann's seminal book *The Crucified God* (SCM Press 1974) is a helpful pointer or corrective. Just as cosmologists cannot know anything about any state of affairs 'before' there was anything to be known, so we cannot know about what it was like for God to be God 'before' the creation. But if we are to speak of mutual love within God 'then', we must at the same time hang onto the unity of God. It was out of this unity that love created. Perhaps, if it is not too crass an illustration, we might think along the lines of what we mean when we say someone is 'at peace with him- or herself'. That state of affairs does not imply that the person has no need of an other to relate to – in fact quite the reverse. Paul S. Fiddes, in his chapter in *The Work of Love*, says, on p. 170, 'if infinite love is a part of God's character as creator, it seems that God will be overflowing with an excess of love that cannot be satisfied within God's own self, even in the communion of the Trinity, but which needs free, responsive beings capable of loving relationships.'

12. Keith Ward, Cosmos and Kenosis, in *The Work of Love, Creation as Kenosis*, ed. John Polkinghorne, published jointly in the United States of America by Wm. B. Eerdmans Publishing Co, and in Great Britain by Society for Promoting Christian Knowledge, 2001, p. 159

13. James Jones, *Jesus and the Earth*, Society for Promoting Christian Knowledge 2003, p. 48

14. Vincent Brúmmer, *The Model of Love*, Cambridge University

Press, 1993, p. 236

Interruption III

1. *Laudato Si,* section 70
2. *Poems and Prose of Gerard Manley Hopkins,* selected with an introduction and notes by W. H. Gardner, Penguin Books, first publ. 1953, p. 30

Chapter 5

1. Richard Crashaw 1613–1649. Anglican cleric and metaphysical poet. Quotation from Lion Christian Quotation Collection BCA 1997 by arrangement with Lion Publishing plc, p. 119. Copyright ©Hannah Ward and Jennifer Wild.
2. James Jones, *Jesus and the Earth,* Society for Promoting Christian Knowledge, 2003, p. 27
3. James Jones, *Jesus and the Earth,* Society for Promoting Christian Knowledge, 2003, p. 7
4. It might be possible to see some connection here to the German philosopher Wittgenstein's concept of 'family resemblance' (*Familienähnlichkeit*). He used the example of 'games', where each game has its own rules, techniques and purposes and so on, but there are overlapping areas between them, so that each game shares with others some but not all characteristics, but all can be filed under the heading 'game'. In the same way, we might think of the subject of a parable and its 'meaning' as sharing a family resemblance – and in this case they would be filed under 'the results of the loving creativity of God'.
5. Edward P. Echlin, *Climate and Christ,* The Columba Press, 2010, pp. 80-81
6. As far as the inevitability of the cross is concerned, we are perhaps used to the idea that Jesus' mission to express God's love and to save those who had walked away from him was from the outset a mission that would lead to his death.

But there is a shadowy hint in Rev 13:8 of a destiny from further back in time – or in fact from before time. The verse introduces the phrase 'from the foundation of the world'. In most translations this is linked to those whose name is written 'in the book of life'. But it can alternatively be linked to 'the Lamb that was slaughtered'. In this case, there is a suggestion that the act of creation itself was already marked by the shadow of the cross. Given what we have thought about the costly nature of love, and how forgiveness is part and parcel of that love, this seems entirely consistent. As others have pointed out, creation is cruciform. Referring to this verse, Christopher Southgate writes that we should avoid the idea 'that the Creator miscalculated and had to send the Incarnate Son as an emergency measure, rather than his coming being the timeless intention of God' (*The Groaning of Creation*, Westminster John Knox Press, 2008, p. 36).

7. Tom Wright, *Surprised by Hope*, Society for Promoting Christian Knowledge, 2007, pp. 74-75

8. Tom Wright, *Surprised by Hope*, Society for Promoting Christian Knowledge, 2007, p. 305. This is from a splendid Tailpiece to the book, satirising two imagined Easter sermons, by 'Pastor Gospelman' and 'Mr Smoothtongue'.

9. James Jones, *Jesus and the Earth*, Society for Promoting Christian Knowledge, 2003, p. 34

Chapter 6

1. William Blake, 1757–1827. From *Auguries of Innocence*. *The Penguin Poets: William Blake*, first publ. 1958, p. 67

2. Information from http://www.wwf.org.uk. The website has a useful and perhaps sobering tool for giving a rough calculation of one's carbon footprint.

3. A report published in October 2017, in the journal *Plos One*, gave the findings of German entomologists who started

collecting data in 1989. They found that in the nature protection areas they studied, the number of flying insects had declined by 76% in 27 years. Mid-summer decline was 82%. The causes are as yet unclear, but more intensive agriculture, with increased use of pesticides and loss of wildflower field margins, is implicated. The report does not see climate change as a direct contributing factor, but it is clearly the case that this decline is taking place whilst global temperatures increase, with all the disturbance to ecosystems that this is provoking.

4. *Laudato Si*, section 193
5. http://www.footprintnetwork.org
6. One could point to the work of A Rocha, Tear Fund, Christian Aid and Green Christian amongst others, as well as the witness of groups such as the Iona Community, with its rediscovery of Celtic Christianity's connection to the created order. But their call has not been taken up by the church at large as a core element of its mission. The Anglican Communion has defined its 'Five Marks of Mission', of which the fifth is indeed 'To strive to safeguard the integrity of creation, and sustain and renew the life of the earth'. This is great, but lofty words do not by themselves reduce the rate of increase of greenhouse gases in the atmosphere.
7. *Laudato Si*, section 217
8. This relates to the guaranteed price per megawatt-hour offered to companies who bid successfully for contracts to build new generating capacity.
9. Information from http://animals.howstuffworks.com/mammals/methane-cow.htm

Chapter 7

1. From his hymn *O praise ye the Lord*.
2. T. S. Eliot, *Little Gidding*, from *Four Quartets*, first published by Faber and Faber Ltd, 1944, reprinted 1968, p. 59

3. Collected Poems of Philip Larkin, edited with an introduction by Anthony Thwaite, first published by The Marvell Press and Faber and Faber Ltd, 2003, p. 117

About the Author

Born in 1947, classical pianist John Blakely received his musical education at The Royal Academy of Music and Balliol College, Oxford. As a chamber musician and accompanist he has performed all over the UK and Europe, and made many commercial recordings, as well as countless live broadcasts and recordings for the BBC. He is a Professor of Piano, Accompaniment and Vocal Repertoire at The Royal College of Music in London.

He is married with three children and eight grandchildren. Besides music and writing, his interests include astronomy, environmental concerns and walking.

As a teacher he enjoys the challenge of using words to explain ideas about music, and of guiding the development of students. He has a particular interest in the psychology of performance, and in finding principles that apply to music of differing styles and periods.

As a writer his aim is to articulate in non-technical language his own explorations in Christian belief and to help others find a way through their struggles with faith. Though based in theology and philosophy, his writing aims to be accessible and practical, so that it can be of pastoral and practical benefit to his readers.

Circle Books

CHRISTIAN FAITH

Circle Books explores a wide range of disciplines within the field of Christian faith and practice. It also draws on personal testimony and new ways of finding and expressing God's presence in the world today.

If you have enjoyed this book, why not tell other readers by posting a review on your preferred book site.

Recent bestsellers from Circle Books are:

I Am With You (Paperback)
John Woolley

These words of divine encouragement were given to John Woolley in his work as a hospital chaplain, and have since inspired and
uplifted tens of thousands, even changed their lives.
Paperback: 978-1-90381-699-8 ebook: 978-1-78099-485-7

God Calling
A. J. Russell

365 messages of encouragement channelled from Christ to two
anonymous "Listeners".
Hardcover: 978-1-905047-42-0 ebook: 978-1-78099-486-4

The Long Road to Heaven
A Lent Course Based on the Film
Tim Heaton

This second Lent resource from the author of *The Naturalist and the
Christ* explores Christian understandings of "salvation" in a five-
part study based on the film *The Way*.
Paperback: 978-1-78279-274-1 ebook: 978-1-78279-273-4

Abide In My Love
More Divine Help for Today's Needs
John Woolley

The companion to *I Am With You*, *Abide In My Love* offers words of
divine encouragement.
Paperback: 978-1-84694-276-1

From the Bottom of the Pond
The Forgotten Art of Experiencing God in the Depths of the Present Moment
Simon Small

From the Bottom of the Pond takes us into the depths of the present moment, to the only place where God can be found.
Paperback: 978-1-84694-066-8 ebook: 978-1-78099-207-5

God Is A Symbol Of Something True
Why You Don't Have to Choose Either a Literal Creator God or a Blind, Indifferent Universe
Jack Call

In this examination of modern spiritual dilemmas, Call offers the explanation that some of the most important elements of life are beyond our control: everything is fundamentally alright.
Paperback: 978-1-84694-244-0

The Scarlet Cord
Conversations With God's Chosen Women
Lindsay Hardin Freeman, Karen N. Canton

Voiceless wax figures no longer, twelve biblical women, outspoken, independent, faithful, selfless risk-takers, come to life in *The Scarlet Cord*.
Paperback: 978-1-84694-375-1

Will You Join in Our Crusade?
The Invitation of the Gospels Unlocked by the Inspiration of Les Miserables
Steve Mann

Les Miserables' narrative is entwined with Bible study in this book of 42 daily readings from the Gospels, perfect for Lent or anytime.
Paperback: 978-1-78279-384-7 ebook: 978-1-78279-383-0

A Quiet Mind
Uniting Body, Mind and Emotions in Christian Spirituality
Eva McIntyre
A practical guide to finding peace in the present moment that will change your life, heal your wounds and bring you a quiet mind.
Paperback: 978-1-84694-507-6 ebook: 978-1-78099-005-7

Readers of ebooks can buy or view any of these bestsellers by clicking on the live link in the title. Most titles are published in paperback and as an ebook. Paperbacks are available in traditional bookshops. Both print and ebook formats are available online.

Find more titles and sign up to our readers' newsletter at http://www.johnhuntpublishing.com/christianity. Follow us on Facebook at https://www.facebook.com/ChristianAlternative.